"Amy has written an inspirational, practical, and must-read book for anyone working with youth or those on the margins. Her faith, transparency, stories, and experiences provide valuable information and insight for connecting with and loving others as Christ loves them."

Karen Swanson, director of the Wheaton College Billy Graham Center Correctional Ministries Institute

"Amy knows high-risk young people, and high-risk young people know Amy. And what they know of each other is seen through the lens of love. That's what makes all the difference, and it's what makes this book so special. Who we become is most deeply influenced by how others see us. And on page after page, Amy illustrates this transformational power of seeing through the eyes of love."

Scott Larson, founder and president of Straight Ahead Ministries

"*Worth Seeing* is well worth reading. Everyone in any kind of ministry should read this book (and that should be all Christians). I have ministered to people on the extreme margins of society for over forty years and gleaned a lot from this book. Amy provides a fresh model for outreach ministry for today's harvest field. She reminds us that the harvest truly is plentiful but the laborers are few, and one plants, one waters, but it is God who gives the increase. I love this book and I think you will too."

Joseph Williams, president of the Nehemiah Consortium

"My sista Amy Williams has created a work of art, a masterpiece, that has taken over thirty years to say! This work of art comes with a life surrendered for those labeled untouchable. We are reading all of Amy's heart, experiencing her blood, sweat, and tears from a life sacrificed for those who felt they had no voice. What you must be ready for is the contagious, tenacious hope that is blanketed in every page. The challenge is 'What ya gonna do about it?' and we must join Amy and create a hope-dealer nation that will nourish the hearts of our youth who are drowning in deserts of hopelessness."

Phil Jackson, founder and CEO of the Firehouse Community Arts Center of Chicago and lead pastor of The House

"Forty-seven years of ministry with and on behalf of court-adjudicated youth and young adults have taught me that the Christian values we seek to impart to them are not sustained without relationships. And biblically based relationships cannot be formed without recognizing the humanity in each other. Amy Williams pens this truth with power and passion. She grounds gripping narrative (hers and others') in a theology of human value to show how many whom society would throw away are yet 'fearfully and wonderfully made.' Ministries like hers helps them to 'know that full well' (Psalm 139:14)! I will be using this book in our criminal justice and reconciliation studies curriculum here in Washington, DC."

Harold Dean Trulear, associate professor of applied theology at Howard University School of Divinity

"My sista Amy Williams, AKA the Hope Dealer, has written one of the most honest, vulnerable, and transformative books I have ever read. You will find yourself experiencing every emotion as you travel with her on a roller coaster ride of heartbreak, healing, and hope. *Worth Seeing* is a powerful reminder that seeing the world the way God does means embracing both the beauty and brokenness in every person and every place."

Jonathan "Pastah J" Brooks, lead pastor of Lawndale Christian Community Church and author of *Church Forsaken*

"This is a great book for those in the field of mentoring and working with youth. It's a look into the real world of the streets from the eyes of a hood hero. I love how Amy uses Scriptures throughout the book. It makes it easier to understand her work with the youth, especially for those who come from a religious background."

Jose, Chicago gang leader

"Amy Williams has gifted us with a book that is full of wisdom, knowledge, and insight rooted in theology, as well as stories full of practicality that can only be given through her genuinely faithful and loving time with high-risk youth. As a chaplain working with incarcerated youth, I'm grateful this book has come at a pivotal time to give me fresh insight, challenges, and reminders of how to minister in God's way—truly seeing one another as God sees us. This book will remain close by for reference as I do ministry. Thank you for being an example for us all!"

Eric G. Peng, Good News Global chaplain at Cook County Juvenile Temporary Detention Center in Chicago

"I met Amy Williams in a tough neighborhood on the West Side of Chicago. She was fearless. Her loud laugh and hope-drenched words sparked something deep inside. The best word I can find is *hope*. Hope for the present and hope for the future. Amy and I have worked together as radio broadcasters and youth leaders. I've seen young men stand tall when she's nearby. They say, 'Amy cares and sees worth in me.' She's a force. I've learned a lot from her. I think you will too."

Roy Patterson, host at Moody Radio

"Amy Williams is an authentic practitioner whose way of life over the last several decades has created a picture of Christ that is compelling and sacred. Amy's devotion to living and loving in the margins is the way of Jesus. This book takes you on a journey of being a Christ-follower. Don't just read Amy's stories. You can embody them. If you want to be inspired and learn what it looks like to be a follower of Christ, then read this book."

Tommy Nixon, CEO of the Urban Youth Workers Institute

VIEWING OTHERS
THROUGH GOD'S EYES

WORTH
SEEING

AMY L. WILLIAMS
A HOPE DEALER

An imprint of InterVarsity Press
Downers Grove, Illinois

InterVarsity Press
P.O. Box 1400 | Downers Grove, IL 60515-1426
ivpress.com | email@ivpress.com

InterVarsity Press® is the publishing division of InterVarsity Christian Fellowship/USA®. For more information, visit intervarsity.org.

Scripture quotations, unless otherwise noted, are from The Holy Bible, English Standard Version, copyright © 2001 by Crossway Bibles, a division of Good News Publishers. Used by permission. All rights reserved.

Scripture quotations marked MSG are taken from The Message, copyright © 1993, 2002, 2018 by Eugene H. Peterson. Used by permission of NavPress. All rights reserved. Represented by Tyndale House Publishers.

While any stories in this book are true, some names and identifying information may have been changed to protect the privacy of individuals.

Figure 1. Steve Parson, *Merciful*, https://steveparson.com, Used with permission.

Figure 2. Adapted from ©David Armano, "Perception Pyramid," *Logic + Emotion* blog, October 16, 2008, https://darmano.typepad.com/logic_emotion/2008/10/perception-pyra.html.

Figure 3. Adapted from "Optical Illusions and How Our Brain Trick Our Eyes," Iris, November 27, 2019, https://iristech.co/optical-illusions.

The publisher cannot verify the accuracy or functionality of website URLs used in this book beyond the date of publication.

Cover design: Lindy Kasler
Cover image: Catherine MacBride/Stocksy
Interior design: Daniel van Loon

ISBN 978-1-5140-0712-9 (print) | ISBN 978-1-5140-0713-6 (digital)

Printed in the United States of America ⊖

Library of Congress Cataloging-in-Publication Data
Names: Williams, Amy L., 1970- author.
Title: Worth seeing : viewing others through God's eyes / Amy L. Williams.
Description: Downers Grove, IL : IVP, [2024] | Includes bibliographical
   references.
Identifiers: LCCN 2024005002 (print) | LCCN 2024005003 (ebook) | ISBN
   9781514007129 (print) | ISBN 9781514007136 (digital)
Subjects: LCSH: Church work with juvenile delinquents. | At-risk
   youth—Pastoral counseling of. | BISAC: RELIGION / Christian Ministry /
   Youth | SOCIAL SCIENCE / Criminology
Classification: LCC BV4464.5 .W526 2024 (print) | LCC BV4464.5 (ebook) |
   DDC 259/.5–dc23/eng/20240226
LC record available at https://lccn.loc.gov/2024005002
LC ebook record available at https://lccn.loc.gov/2024005003

31   30   29   28   27   26   25   24 | 12   11   10   9   8   7   6   5   4   3   2   1

*This book is dedicated to the memory of the first man I
ever loved, my first superhero, and the coolest Black man
I ever met, Foris L. Williams. Forever a daddy's girl.*

*And this book was written because this person
inspires me . . . daily. . . .
To my first best friend, my forever favorite person, my
baby brother Foris "Khalil" Williams II.
You are my hero. More!*

CONTENTS

PART CUATRO—SEEING HOPE

PREFACE

I am beyond excited that you picked up this book and are ready to take this journey with me. I am humbled to welcome you.

Living and serving youth in Chicago is not for the faint of heart. It has been nicknamed "Chiraq, Killinois, Crook County," for a reason. But Chicago has a very special place in my heart. It's the place where my dad grew up, the stories he has shared of his teenage years, the family still there, and the friends that became family. It was where God called me to—regardless of its reputation—or maybe because of it.

I have had the incredible privilege of working with young people since 1994 and, hopefully, will continue for a long time. Most of those years have been spent with youth in gangs and those involved in the criminal justice system, from probation to long jail sentences. Yes, I consider it a great privilege! When young people open up their world to you, a world usually filled with trauma and distrust, it is a privilege. I am thankful for every young person, every gang member, every gang leader, and every incarcerated and formerly incarcerated individual in my

life. I have learned more from them than any other group of people I am connected to. I am always humbled that they trust me with their stories and invite me into their spaces. And I am thankful they invest in me, too—invest their trust, their love, their vulnerability.

Before starting the journey of this book, I want to share a few important points. Though I am a youth worker and make many references to working with youth, this book is for anyone who works with, walks with, and loves people, especially those on the margins. Most principles I discuss can be applied to any work, because the focus is on seeing people through the lens of God. Do not be distracted when I discuss youth work if you're not a youth worker. I am a youth worker, so that's my lens, but I am also surrounded by all kinds of people these principles pertain to as well.

When discussing young people, I am mostly referring to those labeled high-risk youth, who are usually on the margins. My mentor and friend Scott Larson teaches that there is a clear difference between at-risk youth and high-risk youth. Which youth are at risk? *All* youth are at risk, no matter their age, socio-economic background, geographic location, or education level. All youth are at risk of not transitioning to healthy adulthood without outside intervention and other factors. "High-risk youth" are a subset of at-risk youth who, without appropriate outside intervention, will almost certainly inflict damage on themselves, others, or both. These youth face many additional challenges that make it difficult for them to develop into healthy adults without help.

Another point I would like to share is that I personally have never been in a gang or in prison. I do not speak on behalf of those who have been, as I do not share their experience. My goal is to communicate what I have learned from the gang member, the incarcerated individual, the young person, and others. I often attend conferences about these populations and see many panel discussions that do not include them. Why and how? We need to do less talking "about" and talking "at" those on the margins and include them in the conversation. As Just-LeadershipUSA founder Glenn Martin states, "Those closest to the problem are closest to the solution."[1] I am humbled to be a part of the conversation and solution.

Also please note: While all the stories in this book are true, most names and identifying details have been changed to protect the privacy and safety of the people involved.

Ready for the journey? Let's go!

ONE

THE GOD WHO SEES

"You are the God who sees me," for she said,
"I have now seen the One who sees me."

GENESIS 16:13 NIV

"I tried to sell my soul to the devil . . . and he didn't even want it. I'm so damaged."

Luis has pen and paper in his hand, moving to a beat inside his head, writing rap lyrics from inside a small, cold prison cell in Illinois. Writing has become how he spends his days as he serves time awaiting the moment he returns to society and to his nine-year-old son.

"Most of my life, I felt like I was born cursed, unloved. I felt like an outcast from my family and friends."

Born in Puerto Rico in 1993, Luis grew up in Chicago, the baby boy among four brothers and a sister. He loved playing softball and skateboarding, but mostly he loved being with his dad. They were glued at the hip. You never saw one without the other.

Luis didn't know as a child that his father was a functioning heroin addict and a member of a ruthless gang in the neighborhood. All Luis saw was Superman, his best friend, his dad. Then at the young age of ten, he lost his father, and Luis's whole world as he knew it was gone.

"When I lost my pops I lost all hope, and at ten years old, I became my own role model. I wanted to prove to everybody that I can do it all on my own."

Luis was determined to not depend on anyone. They all leave eventually, right? If he didn't get close to anyone again, he couldn't get hurt. He decided he was going to do life on his own.

"I joined the gang when I was nine, a couple months before my dad passed. . . . He didn't know but I wanted to be like him. When he left me, I was alone and felt like I didn't need anybody."

Soon after his father's death, all Luis's brothers joined the same gang, looking for love, protection, a father figure.

"I'm one of the many who grew up in the street and had it all—cars, clothes, money, females, jewelry, all the finer things," said Luis. "But the one thing I didn't have was love or someone who wanted what was best for me. I was looking for that."

And then we met.

Every single time.

I sob huge, extra-wet tears every single time I see that scene in the movie *Freedom Writers*. Erin Gruwell is a first-time history teacher in Long Beach, California, with a class of challenging ninth and tenth graders she is clearly unprepared for. Many of the youth are in rival gangs and fight often in her classroom. As the movie progresses, she finds a way to connect with them relationally and the classroom becomes like a family. The youth publish their stories in a book called *Freedom Writers*, creatively named after the Freedom Riders, the civil rights activists who rode buses across the South protesting the segregation of public transit.

One particular student, Andre Bryant, faces the challenge of being recruited for street life. When his brother loses a court case and faces a lengthy prison sentence, Andre chooses to go back to street life and begins skipping classes. In an assignment, Gruwell's students evaluate themselves on how they feel they're doing in the class. Andre gives himself an F. Gruwell pulls him outside the classroom to ask him why.

He responds, "It's what I feel I deserve, is all."

She looks him square in the eyes with love and fierceness. "I know what you're up against. We're all of us up against some-

> WE ALL WANT TO BE SEEN. WE HAVE A NEED TO BE SEEN.

thing . . . *I see who you are.* I see you. [A tear falls down Andre's face as he fights many more.] Do you understand me? I can see you and you are not failing."

We all want to be seen.

We have a need to be seen.

Not for glory or fame but because of the simple innate human need within us. Being seen makes us feel whole, complete, validated. To live in a world unseen is torture, traumatic. And yet many go unseen daily, especially those on the margins.

To be seen doesn't take much. It can be as simple as an acknowledgment or as huge as an award of recognition. But the

> IT'S ABOUT SEEING AND ACCEPTING THE HUMANITY IN EVERYONE. IT'S ABOUT DISCOVERING OUR OWN WORTH, WHICH ALLOWS US TO SEE THE WORTH IN OTHERS.

seeing I'm talking about goes deeper than surface recognition. It's about seeing and accepting the humanity in everyone. It's about discovering our own worth, which allows us to see the worth in others. Seeing others through the lens of God brings healing and opens our worldview. This requires being (and staying) in the posture of a learner, listening intentionally to understand and validating the story we hear. This formula helps us to develop compassion, and, in turn, compassion requires action.

BUT I UNDERSTAND . . .

In my calling working with youth in gangs and prison, people tend to think I am conflicted.

- I work with the shooter and the one who got shot.
- I work with the thief and the one who got robbed.
- I work with the abuser and the one who got abused.
- I work with the murderer and the family of the murdered.
- I work with the ones who harm and the ones who are harmed.

Yet I never feel conflicted. The way this works for me has been simple: I do not agree with the lifestyle those in gangs have chosen. I do not condone violence or crime. I do not like all that comes with these lifestyle choices. But I *understand.* And understanding leads to mercy and compassion. Once you hear the stories of others, you understand how they have found themselves lost in gang culture, violence, and crime, how they have become lost in abuse, homelessness, and sex work. For some, it's a choice. For others, it's impossible to make any other choice (for example, generational gang membership).

I hope after reading this book the reader will move beyond making assumptions and judgments to listening and developing a connection that leads to deeper understanding, therefore igniting compassion and mercy.

One hot summer afternoon I was driving down a very busy Cicero Avenue. There was dead-stop traffic in both directions, so I was able to see what was going on at the side of the road. A small outreach group of about six church members was outside waving signs and yelling to the traffic, "Stop the Violence," "Put the Guns Down," and "Our Youth Need Us." As I was watching, I noticed two young African American boys walking through the church protesters, and not one protester said anything to them. They walked by without even a hello. Another teen girl walked by in the opposite direction, and no one acknowledged her either. The church members were so busy communicating their message, they failed to see the people the message was for.

Most people on the margins go unseen. The homeless person begging on the street, the gang member posted on the block, the inmate locked away from society, the sex worker on the street corner, the teenager walking down the street. We have become a society that chooses not to look at those on the margins when God is *calling* us to see them. And, as many Black theologians conclude, "There can exist no theology based on the gospel message that does not arise from marginalized communities."[1]

Marginalized communities are "those excluded from mainstream social, economic, educational, and/or cultural life," and marginalization occurs "due to unequal power relationships between social groups."[2] Marginalized groups have less access to services and opportunities. "A person on the margins of a situation or group has very little power, importance, or influence"[3] and receives little to no attention.

A prime example of a person on the margins was Jesus himself. He was among the oppressed, and he fought for the least of these (Matthew 25:40). In *Doing Christian Ethics from the Margins*, Miguel De La Torre explains that "the radicalness of the gospel message is that Jesus was in solidarity with the very least of humanity."[4] As faith believers, this should be true for us as well. But we tend to ignore the invisible. We live in the reality of "outta sight, outta mind," but they're there whether we see them or not. In every city. Every street. Every field. And God is calling us to see them.

SAWUBONA

While walking down the street one fall day, I saw a tall African American boy coming toward me. He had his head down and his long thin dreads were covering his face. I spoke as we passed by each other.

"Hey, how are you doing today?" I kept walking.

He did a double-take and said, "I'm good."

I continued walking to my car. He turned around and said, "Excuse me."

I paused and turned back. "Yeah, what's up?"

"Thank you for saying hi to me. No one ever does that."

I said to him, living out my Erin Gruwell, "I see you, homie. Keep your head up!"

This is the spirit of the African term *sawubona*. This is a common greeting among tribe members and literally means "I see you," but it goes deeper than the physical seeing of a person. This term intends to recognize the worth and dignity of each person. It says, "I see the whole of you—your experiences, your passions, your pain, your strengths and weaknesses, and your future. You are valuable to me."[5] When someone says, "*Sawubona*," your response is supposed to be, "*Shiboka*," which means "I exist for you." This response indicates that someone's full attention is on that person's existence and the value they bring to the world.[6] I imagine this is how God greets us.

The story of Hagar is a great example of this.

HAGAR'S GOD ENCOUNTER

Hagar's story is one of God's pursuit of those who feel unseen, unheard, unloved. In Genesis 16, both Hagar the servant and her mistress Sarai were "desperate for significance, mired in the feeling that the world saw them as deficient."[7]

> Now Sarai, Abram's wife, had borne him no children. She had a female Egyptian servant whose name was Hagar. And Sarai said to Abram, "Behold now, the LORD has prevented me from bearing children. Go in to my servant; it may be that I shall obtain children by her." And Abram listened to the voice of Sarai. So, after Abram had lived ten years in the land of Canaan, Sarai, Abram's wife, took Hagar the Egyptian, her servant, and gave her to Abram her husband as a wife. (Genesis 16:1-3)

During this era, it was not an uncommon practice for women who couldn't bear children to find another woman to have children for the family. The issue here was that God had made a promise to Abram that he would be a father of many generations and have an heir, a son (Genesis 15:4), but Sarai was impatient, like many of us have been a time or twenty. Sarai was embarrassed by her barrenness and gave Abram permission to have Hagar as a surrogate.

> And he went in to Hagar, and she conceived. And when she saw that she had conceived, she looked with contempt on her mistress. And Sarai said to Abram, "May the wrong done to me be on you! I gave my servant to your embrace, and when she saw that she had conceived, she looked on me with contempt. May the LORD judge between you and me!" But Abram said to Sarai, "Behold, your servant is in your power; do to her as you please." Then Sarai dealt harshly with her, and she fled from her. (Genesis 16:4-6)

I'm sure many of us are thinking, "But she said it was okay. It was her idea. Why is she mad?" Jealousy was probably a huge factor here. And since Hagar was an outcast and a servant, Sarai felt validated in her abusive behavior. But Hagar couldn't take the abuse and fled to the desert for an unmentioned amount of time. By cultural standards, she did wrong by running away and leaving her master without his blessing: "Her actions are both illegal and immoral in the context of that culture."[8] But she could no longer withstand the abuse.

> The angel of the LORD found her by a spring of water in the wilderness, the spring on the way to Shur. And he said, "Hagar, servant of Sarai, where have you come from and

where are you going?" She said, "I am fleeing from my mistress Sarai." The angel of the LORD said to her, "Return to your mistress and submit to her." The angel of the LORD also said to her, "I will surely multiply your offspring so that they cannot be numbered for multitude." And the angel of the LORD said to her,

"Behold, you are pregnant
    and shall bear a son.
You shall call his name Ishmael,
    because the LORD has listened to your affliction.
He shall be a wild donkey of a man,
    his hand against everyone
    and everyone's hand against him,
and he shall dwell over against all his kinsmen."

So she called the name of the LORD who spoke to her, "You are a God of seeing," for she said, "Truly here I have seen him who looks after me." (Genesis 16:7-13)

Hagar had an encounter. A God encounter! As a woman and invisible outsider in her culture, to be seen and pursued by the angel of the Lord was a rare experience. Though she was distraught and alone, the angel of the Lord made her feel significant, worthy, and visible. She understood that God was with her and that she had a part in God's plan. God saw her. *All* of her. And she was transformed.

After the encounter, she names God *El Roi*, the God Who

GOD SEES US (INDIVIDUALLY), HE KNOWS US (INDIVIDUALLY), AND HE IS CONCERNED FOR US (INDIVIDUALLY).

Sees. You see this theme throughout the Bible: "that God sees us (individually), that he knows us (individually), and that he is concerned for us (individually)."[9] Hagar's experience is one I want for all of us, especially those society has chosen to write off as useless or worthless. May we all encounter the God Who Sees.

As we walk through this journey together, we will encounter four stages of seeing.

Seeing Myself will give you insight into my journey. As a female gang-intervention specialist and juvenile justice advocate, I have never found it easy to do what I was called to do in this white-male-dominated field. We will explore my story, the challenges, where my need to be seen began, and how, despite resistance, I was able to walk in my purpose.

Seeing Others will challenge you in the mission of seeing the unseen through the lens of God by understanding the importance of story, listening, and validation, as well as the power of perception. We are in the business of seeing people—and seeing them the way God sees them. You will develop skills on expanding your worldview and stretching your limited lens. We will explore gang culture, outreach, trauma, and mentoring that matters.

Seeing Yourself will help us take a look at ourselves as we navigate this complex work of seeing. Before doing the work of seeing others, we must first recognize who we truly are and our role in the kingdom. We can then move forward to seeking and embracing our calling, even using our gift of brokenness, to impact the world.

Seeing Hope will address finding hope in hopeless places and seeing hope flourish in the unexpected. Even in loss there is hope. Seeing hope begins with building relationships, looking for teachable moments, and never losing hope yourself. Seeing hope is being hope to others.

My hope for you throughout this book is that your worldview will be challenged and you will be able to see others, especially those living on the margins, through the eyes of God. After you hear their stories and challenges, may you develop a deeper compassion for others, especially those society tends to label and ignore. I pray that once you put the book down, your heart will explode with mercy for others who need you to see them. I pray the lessons I share will help you move one step closer to seeing others—and yourself—as God sees them.

PART UNO

SEEING MYSELF

TWO

BEST OF BOTH WORLDS

It takes courage to grow up and become who you really are.

E. E. CUMMINGS

Growing up biracial (Irish and Black) in Maine in the 1970s was not easy. Just three years earlier interracial marriage had been illegal, until the ruling of *Loving v. Virginia* in June 1967 changed history. According to the *Portland Press Herald*, in the 1970 census—the first population count after the passage of the 1964 Civil Rights Act—Maine's population was over 99 percent white, and only 2,800 Mainers identified as Black or African American.[1]

My mother's family did not accept her marrying a Black man, nor did society, but my dad's family was supportive and they embraced my mom. I remember my mom telling me that when

we were younger, someone stopped to ask her if she was baby-sitting. Biracial children weren't the norm. I didn't see Black kids growing up in Maine. I saw white kids and a few biracial kids sprinkled here and there. My worldview was limited regardless of how hard my parents tried to show me a broader perspective.

In June of 1972, my mother brought home a little baby boy. After playing with him for a few days, I told her she could "take him back now." Little did I know my baby brother, Skip, would become my first best friend and I would *never* want to return him. With only a two-year age difference, I don't know if a brother-sister team could have been closer than the two of us were as kids. Growing up in New England, and then doing teenage life in North Carolina, we didn't have much, but we had each other, and we counted on that. You couldn't separate us growing up.

We were so close that my brother was hospitalized one day because of it. In 1985, I went on a ninth-grade field trip to Washington, DC. I was beyond excited to travel with my friends and get away on my own. It was the first trip that would separate my brother and me for days at a time. That weekend he broke out in hives all over his body. Mom rushed him to the hospital for treatment. The doctor didn't know where the hives came from, but my mom knew it was his nerves and separation anxiety. When I called home that night, I found out the news and freaked out. I needed to get home right away! But Mom was not letting that happen. I finished my trip in DC in anxiety, wanting to rush home so he wouldn't have hives anymore. It was all my fault. When I got home, I rushed through the door to hug my brother tight, apologizing profusely. We made a promise we would never separate again and would buy houses next door to each other and live happily ever after. He now lives in a different city in

California, and I'm in Chicago—he's the farthest next-door neighbor I've ever had.

My parents divorced in 1975 when I was four years old. Growing up in an alcoholic environment (both mother and father being functional addicts) impacted us greatly. I was blessed to have my dad always in my life. He was the coolest Black man on this planet. We visited him every other weekend when we lived in Maine and every summer when we moved to North Carolina. He made sure we knew our Black heritage, mostly through family stories and music.

My dad loved music. He could play any instrument, but his greatest love was for the bass guitar. He started an a cappella group called Street Corner Symphony with my uncle Fred, cousin Buggy, and family friend Sugar Bear. Every weekend they would sing in the basement with kids running around, clapping, dancing, and trying to sing like their daddies. It was the best of memories. Music and my dad. He was the one who introduced us to the life-changing culture of hip-hop in 1981. He played "Rapper's Delight" and "Double Dutch Bus" on a car ride during one of his pickup weekends, and my brother and I were changed forever in a single moment, a single beat.

Living and growing up in Maine, I was in a unique situation where the only couples I saw around my dad were Black men with white women. This was my normal, and I loved seeing, on the weekends, children and babies who looked like me. I didn't feel out of place when I was with my dad. But I still knew I was different. I vaguely remember one day in elementary school being bullied because I was biracial. Though I don't remember all the details, I do remember my mom's response to it. She boldly and lovingly said to me, "You are the best of both worlds. You are Black *and* white and beautiful. If anyone has a problem with that, that is *their* problem, not yours. There is nothing wrong with you. That's what makes you special. You're the lucky one."

Something clicked in me that day and I have not been the same since. The validating words of my mother empowered me to fully embrace my identity and ethnicity. Those words gave me the strength to confront anyone who challenged my identity. After that, I never internalized anyone's issue with me being biracial but walked in great pride that I was "the best of both worlds." From there, the boldness in my character grew. I became a different Amy that day.

■ ■ ■

My mom remarried in 1978, and Eddie became a bonus dad to us. We left Maine in 1982 to be near his family in Greensboro, North Carolina. Leaving my dad behind in Maine was painful for both me and my brother but my brother was excited to be around people of color, the culture, the music. He jumped right in. But moving to the South was a huge culture shock for me.

I was overwhelmed by how many Black people there were in Greensboro, but it also felt like a whole new world opening up to me. My first best friend in North Carolina, Lisa Fowler, was biracial, allowing me to stay with what I knew. We both were children of color with white mothers, and we didn't see much of that in North Carolina. I had hazel eyes and long hair, and I was bullied by Black girls for the way I looked. I didn't understand that, because I couldn't help how I looked. I wasn't accepted, but that didn't stop me. Remember? I was the best of both worlds! My friend group consisted of kids who were Asian, white, Middle Eastern, and Black, but I mostly hung around my brother and his friends. They accepted me as a homie, and my brother protected me. I wanted to be friends with whoever accepted me as

I was, with people who saw me—until a conversation with my favorite eighth-grade teacher made me think about my place in society.

During lunch, I usually sat with my diverse group of friends. But one day, one of my Black friends asked me to sit with her group, all Black females. I was nervous because my experience with Black girls had not been a positive one. But when I looked over to their table, they were all waving for me to come over. I joined them and had a blast! As I was laughing, my teacher came over and whispered in my ear, "It's about time you started hanging out with your own kind."

Instant confusion. My own kind? These girls weren't my own kind. I was more like the mix of cultures at the other table. But being so young, looking for my identity and place, I realized society saw me as a little Black girl. And maybe these were my people? After that, I ate lunch only with my Black girlfriends, even though I never felt fully myself or fully accepted.

I WANTED TO BE FRIENDS WITH WHOEVER ACCEPTED ME AS I WAS.

Growing up, I was always the "good" girl. From elementary school to high school, I was the straight-A student, president of this club, leader of that club, in every play and every talent show. I participated in everything at school. My brother, on the other hand, was all about his music and his friends.

When we were teenagers, Skip's decision to associate with a group of close friends who engaged in criminal behaviors impacted my life in a way I never thought possible. He had access to the same resources I did and a family who loved him, but he also had a lot of trauma and anger. He got involved in some shady activity that caused my mom to send him to Maine in 1986 to live with my dad and his wife, Willow, in hopes of not losing him to the streets. The intervention didn't work, and he moved back to North Carolina in 1987 with us. By this time, my mom was divorced from my stepdad and deeper in her addiction.

While I was a sophomore in college in 1989, my mom went to back to Maine to get sober. She left my brother in North Carolina to finish his last year of high school. Instead, my brother got deeper into the drug-dealing lifestyle, which involved guns and lots of enemies. After a drive-by shooting incident, my mother moved my brother back to Maine to live with my dad while she continued her treatment.

Unfortunately, my brother had a close friend in Maine who led him straight back to the streets. This caused many issues with my dad and his wife. The only decision they came up with was to drop my brother off at the YMCA at the age of seventeen to live life on his own terms. To this day, I have never been okay with that decision. The trauma it caused my brother still affects him deeply today as an adult. It also caused him as a teen to look to the streets for his survival. My brother got into some legal trouble and fled Maine with his best friend to Los Angeles. Life got even harder there, and he eventually joined a gang and spent many years in and out of prison for various types of crime. He was deep in the gang life and soon became addicted to the very product he was selling. His gang became his family, and he would do anything for them, even the things that put his own life in danger.

During the years between 1992 and 1994, I often didn't know if my brother was dead or alive. The tears I cried were filled with pain, regret, and fear. Either I didn't know where he was or we had minimal contact. It was horrifically painful. I felt helpless. Those years caused anxiety and trauma for me and for his newborn daughter, Amber, who was conceived during a short visit to North Carolina in 1993. During that visit, I was very arrogant and pushy with my brother about being saved (it's what I was being taught). I wanted him to be free and healed, but instead, I was the reason he was turned off from Christianity, even to this day. He needed to see the God of love, mercy, and grace but I couldn't be for him what I never received from this church myself.

Over these years I tried everything I could to "save" my brother—send money, house him when I could, pay rent, encourage him, pray and pray harder, try to get him to leave Cali to connect with his daughter—anything I could do with the limited resources I had. I would give him money so he wouldn't be homeless before I would pay my own rent. He was my best friend, and I was broken by what was happening to him. But there was nothing I could do to rescue him—and he wasn't ready to be rescued.

THREE

BECOMING A HOPE DEALER
TO THE DOPE DEALER

When it comes to this gospel, I got no chill for real,
I could teach you how to hope deal.

WORD SMITH

I never wanted to be in ministry. Ever.

And never did I imagine God's plan for my life would be to walk alongside youth in gangs and the criminal justice system, especially as a woman. Why me? *How* me? I already had a plan. I thought it was a pretty good plan too. My dream was to live a simple life: marriage, at-home mom (not so simple), a house on the beach in North Carolina. But here I am, some three decades

later, in full-time ministry: divorced, no kids, in the hood in Chicago. God had a whole other life for me. So how did I get here?

I didn't grow up around religion. My mom dabbled here and there, but we were never committed to anything. In 1987 when I was in high school, I experimented with Christianity because of my friend Kieta, but I never really knew what it all meant. It's just what her family did on Sundays.

I made the decision to completely follow God in August 1992 at the age of twenty-one. There was no magic moment or traumatic event that led me to this decision. My initial understanding of following God was that I would be a member of a church, attend on Sunday mornings, pray once a day, and that was it. I did not realize I would be entering into a deep, loving, life-changing relationship with God. No one ever told me about that. No one told me it would be a transformational relationship.

The first church I joined in 1992 was a deep southern Black Pentecostal church in Durham, North Carolina. The no-makeup, women-in-skirts, no-earrings kind of Pentecostal church. The music was amazing, the pastor could preach us all out of our seats, the people there were "saved saved." I drove forty-five minutes one way five days a week (because if you missed one day, you were a backslider). I immediately began volunteering and helping in any way I could. I was a sponge and absorbed everything I was told, believed everything I was told, and, eventually, was hurt by almost everything I was told.

The church loved both the Lord and the pastor as if they were one and the same. I allowed the pastor to dangerously control me because I wanted to please the Lord. I wanted to get into heaven. I wanted to be special . . . I wanted God to see me. This church taught a lot of manmade doctrine that trained me to be judgmental and super-righteous. This caused many problems in my relationships (especially with my brother), but I didn't know any better. I just did what I was taught, all in an effort to be accepted, loved, and seen.

I remember the first time I started questioning what I was being taught. My husband at the time had tickets to a 1995 Duke-versus-Carolina basketball game that we weren't able to use. We thought it would be nice to give the tickets to our pastor. As I was getting the house ready for him to stop by, I had on my favorite sweatpants that I wore when I got home from work. I was anxious and wondered if I should put on a skirt since the pastor was coming over. My husband proclaimed, "This is our home. That's what you wear here. It's okay to keep them on."

I was nervous and uncomfortable, but I kept them on at my husband's encouragement. When the pastor came to the door, I immediately apologized for wearing sweatpants. "I'm not going to get into trouble for wearing pants, am I?"

The pastor laughed and said, "As long as you wear them inside and no one sees you."

I was shocked! It was all for show? For others to see? What about God? And that was the beginning of me questioning everything I was taught under his leadership. My eyes were opened to how much nonbiblical doctrine I was following, and then my journey changed forever.

My ex-husband was definitely called to ministry. As soon as we married in 1994, we were thrust into his calling. As a former Duke basketball standout and an overall good man, my ex had always been in the limelight and was well-known and very much liked by everyone who met him. Because of that, he was able to start preaching, and we started the Christian Basketball Academy. In 1997, he was being recruited by Young Life to start an urban chapter in Durham. I remember the day we approached our pastor (the same pastor we gave basketball tickets to) to share that we were going into ministry full-time. His response was, "Well, God didn't tell me you were called. Until—and if—he does, you're not allowed to take the job." We were shocked and deflated. Why would God have to tell him before he told us? We wrestled for months, but we couldn't ignore what God had called us to.

While Young Life Urban patiently waited for our decision, they invited us to the regional staff retreat at Windy Gap, a beautiful camp in the mountains of North Carolina. Yes, I wore a skirt. They had on pants and shorts . . . and there were so many white people. This was going to be a challenge. Once we arrived, we were greeted with love and excitement. I had never felt so welcomed anywhere in my life. We started the weekend with a worship session. I had never heard worship music like that or seen so many people in shorts and T-shirts calmly singing and crying to the Lord. I was so busy watching them I couldn't even worship. I loved all of it, though I didn't understand it. I was conditioned that worship was loud and emotional—and long. We were done in twenty minutes. Had we really worshiped if it was that short and calm?

As the weekend continued, I heard about something I never knew existed during the three years I had been serving the Lord: *grace.* They talked about grace, they breathed grace, they were examples of grace. What I understood grace to be at the time was the freedom in God to make mistakes and wrong decisions, to not be perfect, and to know that no matter what, he still loves you, uses you, and accepts you.

That's not what I'd been taught. I'd been taught you must earn God's favor and love, and doing wrong brings his (and others') judgment and wrath upon you. I'd been taught that heaven is the goal but hell is what you might get at any moment. I'd been taught performance-based Christianity, and it was heavy. It was overwhelming. It was exhausting. I judged everybody who wasn't "performing" like me (non-Christians especially), and I never felt like my true self. I was becoming someone I didn't like. I wasn't enjoying life, but as long as God was pleased with my works, happiness didn't matter.

That weekend I was set free. I wanted *that* God. I began a journey of unlearning much of the theology and doctrine I had been taught. I am forever grateful for Young Life Urban and the example of grace they taught me.

After that weekend, we left the Pentecostal church and went on staff full-time with Young Life Urban . . . freely.

I didn't think I would survive. The years 2000 and 2001 were the hardest of my life. It started with my husband of five years deciding to take a job in New York and not telling me until the day he left, leaving me alone, hyperventilating as he packed his clothes around me. He abandoned me, the marriage, and his life in North Carolina. While I was struggling through that loss, my seven-year-old niece and the love of my life, Amber Jean Williams, died in a car accident on December 21, 2001. With all the other losses I was experiencing at the time (the death of my favorite uncle, the September 11 tragedy, loss of my job, finding out my husband was cheating on me, being served divorce papers by a sheriff, and more), I was most devastated by the death of my niece, the most precious person to me in my life.

She showed me what it was like to be seen and unconditionally loved, like God showed Hagar.

All these events led to a decision to start over and move to Chicago in October 2003 to be close to family and my many Chicago friends . . . and to be clear, I was through with ministry! I even purposely bought a small two-door Acura sports coupe because it was too small to transport youth. All I wanted was a simple life—a job downtown, a church for Sundays only, hanging out with friends, and enjoying the city. But again—as always—God had other plans. He let me live that life for about a year as I healed from the losses I experienced in North Carolina.

In 2004, I was attending a Latino church on the North Side of Chicago. My plan was to attend on Sundays only and make some new friends. That's it. I was not going to volunteer, work, or serve at the church. Just get my worship on, receive the Word, and keep it moving. But no matter how hard I tried, I kept being drawn to the young people . . . and they were drawn to me. After church, young people would come to me and ask for advice, hang out, or just get a hug. The adults never did that with me. After a few months, one of the young people asked me to attend their youth night worship service . . . and that was it. I was sucked in. That was the start of a new beginning. The Lord got me again. And now I was a biracial youth leader at a Latino church, not knowing there would be many challenges ahead.

One of the youth invited a friend who was involved in a gang and asked me if I would talk to him, because she felt I could reach him. At this time, the theology I was being taught was, "Get as many to the Lord as you can. That's your goal. The more you bring to Jesus, the more likely you are to get into heaven." I had tunnel vision. My only goal was to get young people to Jesus—but I was not a fan of how this church was doing it. They seemed to be more of a repellent for youth who didn't know the Lord.

The senior pastor saw my heart for youth outside of the church and assigned me to start a small group for them. I started G-Phi-G (Glori-Phi-God) with more opposition than support from the youth ministry. My group consisted of youth who were in gangs, LGBTQ, tired of the church they grew up in, practicing witchcraft, and so on. We became a tight-knit family.

As a woman in leadership at this church, I was allowed only certain privileges, like only praying for the girls and not being able to teach during services. It wasn't long after I challenged the rules and started successfully leading a group of youth that I was "encouraged" to take time off because I was "breaking the rules." During the two months I was gone, no one from the church reached out to me—not even the youth pastor whose leadership I was under. The senior pastor even scolded me and said, "I trusted you with this group when I could have had you cleaning toilets instead."

I knew I would never be seen as more than a woman, never as a leader. I left the church and so did the youth who were with me. That broke my heart, as I encouraged them to stay. They shared with me that they saw how I was being treated and didn't trust the youth pastor or leadership after that. I feel bad to this day, but I understand.

In 2005, I heard about a church that seemed too good to be true. I had to see it for myself. It was called The House, Chicago's first hip-hop church led by Pastor Phil Jackson. Church *and* hip-hop? Soon after I began attending and volunteering, I was hired part-time at The House. I also became a youth pastor at The Carpenter's House, a predominately Latino church in Humboldt Park. I was also attending the fifteen-month DeVos Urban Leadership Initiative Chicago cohort. I had my hands full. I was loving and walking life with young people *full-time*. I was learning how to impact lives, I was teaching young people about the Bible and justice issues, and I was being seen as a formidable force in the youth ministry circle . . . but something wasn't right. Something was missing.

I loved being a youth pastor, but in 2007 I realized I was becoming someone I didn't recognize or like. My heart, my DNA, my passion was always for youth who would never walk through a church door on a Sunday, youth on the margins, youth who gave church the middle finger, young people who were rarely paid attention to. But here I was pastoring youth who grew up in the church.

It didn't fit. No matter how hard I tried to create a ministry that was for both types of youth, the church wasn't supportive. I felt more like a babysitter than a youth pastor. The senior pastor understood what I was trying to do, but he was under the direction of the board and other pastors and a congregation of old-school followers.

One day I was teaching a Bible study and I found myself snapping at the youth. I noticed it myself, but I couldn't stop. I ended the Bible study early and pulled a friend over to the side. In tears, I expressed how frustrated I had been lately and I could see I was taking it out on the youth I cared about. I didn't want to do this youth pastoring anymore, and I didn't know why.

My friend simply said to me, "Maybe you're frustrated because you're doing something God didn't tell you to do."

I snapped at him. "I know what God has called me to do. He called me to love and walk life with young people."

"Then why are you so frustrated?" he asked.

I walked away mad at him. I couldn't believe he'd said to my face I shouldn't be a youth pastor anymore. How dare he!

I thought I could walk away from that conversation and be mad at him forever, but that conversation stuck with me. I was too defensive to consider that maybe there was something to it. The truth was I wasn't supposed to be there *for that long*. In the beginning, God showed me I was there to get it started, not stick around for the long haul—and I was disobedient. I was comfortable. I was going with the flow. But that flow was hurting the youth I loved so much. I met with the pastor and stepped down from my position. I knew my heart was in the streets, in the prisons, on the blocks. But what now?

Months later, a simple afternoon of prayer turned into a life-changing encounter. The conversation went something like this:

Me: "So, God, what do you want me to do now?"

God: *I need you to move into a gang neighborhood.*

Me (after a long pause): "You got jokes! That is funny!"

I know most of you immediately do what God tells you do, but not me. I ask questions. Lots of questions. My thinking was, "I'm too beautiful to move into a gang neighborhood. They would all want to date me! I mean, I am too fly." But God humbled me, reminded me I wasn't that fly and that I needed to do this one thing: *I am not asking you to go into the hood and save anyone. I don't see any nails in your wrists or sides. I haven't left that neighborhood or abandoned them either. Those are my people. But what I am asking is for you to be a light in a kid's darkness.*

That's all it took, and the search for a new apartment was on!

I looked at so many apartments that July. So. Many. Apartments. I could be a realtor with all the knowledge I accumulated!

One day I went to see an apartment in the Humboldt Park community on Beach and Spaulding. I had no idea at the time that this block was well-known as the birthplace of a huge Latino gang. At the time, this block was number two in the most shootings in the city of Chicago. I had no idea. Didn't really care, honestly.

The building I visited had no one living in it, and the realtor was not going to meet me there. He had a lockbox for this particular apartment. When I arrived to look, there were several youth sitting on the porch. I struck up a conversation with them and we all went inside to check out the place (thinking back, that probably wasn't a good idea). I immediately clicked with three of the youth, especially Trey. I asked them about the neighborhood, and they didn't recommend it for a "woman like you." We ended up hanging out for an hour as Trey introduced me to everyone on the block. I immediately felt at home. *This* is it. *This* is the neighborhood I want to impact!

There was an apartment I loved on Evergreen (two streets south of Beach), but I couldn't stand the shower in the bathroom. I kept looking for other apartments, but nothing. For some reason, the apartment I loved wouldn't rent out. The landlord said every applicant was a bust. I had two days before my current lease was up, and I really had no other choice except this apartment with the shower I hated. I went to visit one last time in the evening.

After the visit I sat on the stoop to think about it. I noticed something I hadn't seen before: in the yard was a lamppost, the only one on the whole street. It was shining so bright I couldn't even look right at the light. As I was seeing this, I remember the Lord calling me to be a *light in a kid's darkness*. The search for a new apartment had ended. I found my neighborhood, and a hope dealer to the dope dealer was born.

■ ■ ■

Coined by Christian rapper Word Smith, the term *neighborhood hope dealer* became a well-known phrase in the Christian community. I was on the block with some of my youth and threw out the phrase. One of my youth excitedly said, "That's you, Miss Amy! You're a hope dealer to us." From that moment on (and considering the population I serve), I embraced the nickname, and it has followed me since.

WHAT IS A HOPE DEALER?

In every workshop I teach, I show this image of *Merciful* by Steve Parson and ask, "Tell me what you *see* in this picture." Many point out the obvious—a gun, a thug, Jesus, a crossroads. Others see acceptance, compassion, mercy, forgiveness, and love.

My next question is, "Tell me what you *feel*."

The audience gets quiet as they get in tune with themselves. I have had many cry, many fail to find words, and others share they feel love, shame (on themselves), joy, and hope. Yes, hope.

Every time I see this picture, I am moved. I am moved to great emotion and moved to action. It is a reminder of why I do what I do and a reminder of my prayer for every kid I encounter: *hope in Jesus Christ*. The hope is that anyone can come as they are, that he will not turn you away but embrace, love, and forgive you. It's a picture of hope for the one who thinks he is alone and not worth a second, third, or millionth chance. The artist intentionally made the image of Jesus the same skin color as the young man to teach people that *you* are created in his image, *you*

Figure 1. *Merciful*, created by Steve Parson

are a reflection of him, *you* were created for a purpose greater than the choices you may have made.

So, what is a hope dealer?

- A hope dealer sees everything in this picture and more.
- A hope dealer can see past the image a person presents to see the image of God in them.

- A hope dealer believes in the possibility and potential of every person, no matter what it looks like, because hope dealers themselves are counting on that same hope.

- A hope dealer is willing to go where needed (where most fear to go) and do what it takes to be a light in someone's darkness. Drug dealers do! So why do we shrink at the thought of reaching out to the same people?

- A hope dealer doesn't just deal hope but walks life with people as the hope manifests itself in their hearts, minds, and paths.

- A hope dealer understands that, until someone is ready, *we* are the example of Christ's chase-them-down-pursuing-them-at-all-costs kind of love.

- But mostly, a hope dealer knows hope and peace can be found only in, through, and from God—not in anything we do or say. Our hope is that we are forgiven, we are loved, and we have a purpose that only we can fulfill.

FOUR

TO BE SEEN OR NOT TO BE SEEN

*Most people would trade everything they know, everyone
they know—they'd trade it all to know they've been seen, and
acknowledged, that they might even be remembered.*

DAVE EGGERS

"We're used to being watched. We're not used to being seen."

Father Greg Boyle, founder of gang-intervention ministry
Homeboy Industries, made this comment during a conference
I attended in Chicago, and it has resonated with me ever since.

All most of us ever want in life is to be good enough, to be
accepted as we are. This has been the core spiritual struggle
of my entire life. To this day I have moments of not feeling

good enough—when dating, when speaking and training, when alone at night with my thoughts. Why is this such a struggle for me?

In 2002, I saw a *Dr. Phil* episode that changed my life and led me into my healing journey. It finally clicked. I learned where the root that caused me to question my worth—even as an adult—had been planted in my spirit as a child.

I was a little girl, probably eight or nine, when my mom and I were in the kitchen. We lived on an old farm and there was a beautiful black potbelly stove with a fresh loaf of baked bread sitting on top. I can almost smell it now. I asked my mom a question about my dad and the conversation took an unexpected turn. The conversation centered around the difficulty of biweekly visits. In that one moment, that one conversation, the kingdom of darkness planted a seed I would base my identity on: *I am worthy only if I am chosen. Who I am isn't good enough. I need to be* better *to be chosen.*

At that moment the little girl decided she had to be perfect—to be good enough for her dad so he would *choose* her. That was the keyword. I needed him to choose me to prove I was worthy. I became the "good girl" and performed with excellence at everything to prove myself to him. This was also how I became toward all men—needing to prove I was good enough.

I look back at many of my relationships (Mom wouldn't let me date until I was fifteen—thanks so much for that, Mom!), and I see how that childhood moment shaped what I believe about relationships even to this day. I used to pursue boys who had girlfriends or boys who didn't want me, because if they *chose* me, I was good enough. My worth would be fulfilled for a short period until I needed to pursue another boy to get a renewed sense of validation and worth.

Several times in my teen years my dad chose his wife over his children, and each time that little girl inside me was devastated. She would wrestle with her worth and find ways to prove it to him again and again. Did my dad see me?

As a young adult, I had a healing conversation with my dad where I shared my hurt and struggles. We healed together that day, and our relationship blossomed in my young adulthood. But the struggle of my worth is still with me.

I have realized that this is also how I see God. Our relationship with our heavenly Father is directly connected to the relationship we have with our earthly father. According to Matthew Brown, "Sociologists say it's common for people to perceive that God is like the fatherly figure in their lives. If dad is caring, patient, and concerned, then children will believe God has those same characteristics. And the opposite holds true when a father is harsh, judgmental or absent."[1]

As I examine my relationship with God, I see the direct correlation between how I saw my dad and the things I have needed to relearn about God. That devastated little girl believed God saw her worth only if he chose her. So as a young Christian, I thought I had to perform, to be perfect, and God would choose me. That made the Pentecostal church a perfect fit since it was works-based. When God didn't choose me, the little girl would crawl into a corner and try to figure out what I did wrong. The burden was on me. Why wasn't I good enough?

Throughout my childhood and college years, I didn't know my mom and dad were addicted to alcohol. I do not recall one moment seeing them drunk. They were functional alcoholics. They could get along in society but were controlled by their unmanageable craving to drink. I remember my parents coming home from work, pouring a drink or two, and sipping on it all night. It was as normal as me drinking Kool-Aid after school.

I am glad I was not exposed to a wild, abusive alcoholic life-style, but there were still many repercussions of being raised by two alcoholics. I myself have never been drunk and I am not a drinker, whereas my brother inherited the addiction. But just because I am not addicted to alcohol doesn't mean I don't have addictive behaviors.

One thing I learned early was the alcoholic's mantra: Don't talk, don't trust, don't feel. It was about keeping the peace in the family and not ruffling Mom's feathers. Whatever she said, whatever she felt, that was the way it was. This gave me little space to have my own thoughts, beliefs, and feelings that I could share openly—and I didn't mind because it kept Mom and the house peaceful. It wasn't until I was older that I realized the impact this had on my life.

In the 1990s, basketball was my life. I loved everything about it—until I didn't. I was married to a Duke University basketball star, and everywhere we went, we were stopped and asked for a picture, an autograph, a conversation. My ex was a good man and the funniest man I had ever met. That's what made me fall in love with him. We dated in college, reunited years later, and married six months after that. We were young and free when we married. I was twenty-three and he was twenty-five, but we knew we had found the one—or at least the one who fit the description of what we both thought marriage was at the time.

Looking back, I realize he married me because he wanted a trophy wife. He wanted the life of the rich and famous, a nice car, a nice house, and a beautiful wife. He needed to perpetuate the idea that he had his life together at all times. I was just an object to make him look good.

In my journey of healing after the divorce, I realized one major reason I married him: I needed to be good enough. If someone as well-known as him *chose* me, the empty hole would be filled. I wanted to be somebody, and marrying him would accomplish that. I was looking to my ex to do what only God could do. The pressure on him wasn't fair, but at the time I couldn't name the dark hole inside to realize I was putting that pressure on him.

At the beginning of the marriage, it was fun. It was great to be noticed by the public and friends. Everyone was kind. Always laughing and smiling around us. It was also fake, but we kept moving through it. But I soon learned that being noticed is not the same as being seen. People knew my face and last name, but no one saw Amy (or knew my first name). They saw what I could do for them and who I knew, but they didn't see the young lady who wanted to make a difference in the world. It was lonely for both of us. I often felt pain for my husband, who'd had to navigate that experience since he was a teenager. Unfortunately for us, we also stopped "seeing" each other, and our marriage ended with my husband's desperate need to be seen as worthy enough in the basketball community. They took him in and he left me behind . . . alone.

I turned thirty years old in the midst of my husband leaving me. I decided I wanted to celebrate it in a big way despite how I was feeling. I picked myself up and went to Chicago for a week. My best friend at the time, Melanie, who was now living there, made the week special and unforgettable. I did something fun every day of the week, from a full spa day to salsa dancing to eating at some great ethnic restaurants. I spent that Thursday evening with my dear friend Ted. He took me to the Signature Room (the ninety-sixth floor of the historic John Hancock building), and we ended the evening at my favorite spot in the city, the museum campus where you can see the whole Chicago skyline lit up at night.

We talked for hours about everything . . . and then a conversation took place that changed my world, my life, my ministry. I don't remember the topic of conversation, but I remember Ted's response to something I'd said: "I can see why you think that. I don't quite see it that way, but you are entitled to what you believe."

I paused for a moment because I didn't know what I was feeling. I had to think about it. I was a thirty-year-old woman, and this was the first time someone had disagreed with me without a fight and let me believe what I did, even if they didn't believe the same.

I. Was. Seen. Not for the first time, but this time was different.

I never really knew what validation was until then. Remember what I was taught: Don't talk. Don't trust. Don't feel. Ted's validation made me feel seen and heard. My whole world opened up as a result of that one conversation. I could actually have my own beliefs. I didn't need to believe what everyone else believed just to keep the peace. I could stand on the confidence that it was okay not to agree with everyone else.

This changed the way I interacted with people, especially young people. No longer was I going to force what I believed down people's throats with the objective of being right. No longer was I going to unfriend people I didn't agree with. No longer was I going to shut people down for believing differently than me. I was going to validate others and use it as my key tool in connecting with young people. I am forever grateful to Ted for impacting my life in such a powerful way. I am thankful to God for teaching me this, because it would become the main tool I used in ministry to allow others to be themselves.

I have been a dancer my whole life, thanks to my mom. When I was a child, almost every Saturday morning, after we did chores, she would partner dance with me. I look back at that time now and love our special bond that carried me into the dance world. I was a break dancer, hip-hop dancer, ballet dancer, modern dancer. You name it, I tried it. My brother and I would enter dance contests together as children and always won first place. I was in every talent show in junior high and high school. Dance was my passion, a huge part of who I was growing up.

But all that came to a halt in 1994 when the Pentecostal church I joined told me dancing was a sin. I gave up a huge part of who I was to be what I thought God wanted me to be. I felt a huge hole in my heart, but I was told God would fill that and create a new being and passion in me . . . but dance was in my DNA.

As I was going through my divorce in 2001, I took a trip to Tampa to spend some time with Melanie, who was living there at the time. She was a beautiful, proud Puerto Rican woman who was also going through a marriage struggle. One day we had spent the whole day talking and crying. After such an emotional day she exclaimed, "We need to go out and go salsa dancing!"

I was a little nervous, but at that point of my journey I was challenging everything I'd been taught by this pastor . . . and I trusted Melanie. I mean, David danced. Why couldn't I? I had no idea how to dance salsa, so I thought I would just watch her while sipping on a Pepsi. I saw her. I was mesmerized! The music made my heart beat faster. It was lively, the rhythms forced my body to move; the eclectic clave beat, conga drums, bongos, and timbales made my head spin. Melanie was floating on air as she was led across the dance floor. Her joy was contagious. I wanted to learn that!

Several men had asked me to dance but I didn't know how to do this elegant dance. Melanie had her friend come over to ask (teach) me to dance, and he was very patient with me. One, two, three. Five, six, seven. Quick, quick, slow. Quick, quick, slow. And spin! I was hooked! Something in me woke up. I hadn't felt this alive in years! I couldn't stop smiling. I couldn't stop moving. I wanted to dance and dance and learn this salsa. I felt like a new version of me had been birthed, and this started my obsession with dancing again.

Going through a tough divorce in 2001, I was feeling less than, not beautiful, lifeless and empty. But salsa dancing made me feel connected, sexy, beautiful, alive. God allowed me to find that part of Amy I had forsaken, and it helped me in my healing process. Salsa dancing saved my life. It was through dancing that I found myself connecting with the Latino culture and being fully accepted by them.

All my life, I wasn't white enough. I wasn't Black enough. But in the Latino culture, I was enough. I was accepted. I felt seen. I call myself a "Sorta Rican" since I look Puerto Rican, and many embrace me as such. Even when I tell people I am not Latina, after the shock wears off and I share my ethnicity, I am still greeted with love. This was the community God called me to so I could heal. When I moved to Chicago, it was only natural for me to live close to Melanie (who relocated from Tampa to Chicago) in Humboldt Park, Chicago's Puerto Rican community. I felt at home.

Everyone who knows me knows my deep love and appreciation for the Latino culture. When moving to Chicago, I was able to explore that culture fully and fell in love even more. Every church I attended was Latino (predominantly Puerto Rican), and when I finally found my "home" at The Carpenter's House in Humboldt Park, I was even more convinced I was supposed to be ministering to youth in that culture and context. I came on as the youth pastor, and I jumped right in. I was high energy all the way and motivated to make disciples and reach out to those in the streets and prisons. I had a plan—and the kids loved it. The parents weren't quite sure what to expect, especially with my mission of outreach. I wanted to create a youth ministry that would minister both to youth who grew up in the church and youth who had no desire to know God. Unfortunately, I couldn't get leadership on board with that, only the senior pastor. I was on fire . . . then the flame was reduced to a flicker with one conversation.

"You know this is a Latino church," the senior pastor explained. "And being that you're not Latina, you'll have to tone it down and figure out how to fit in until they can fully accept you."

Everything in me had to hold it together. I wanted to cry. I wanted to scream. I wanted to run out the door. I wanted to quit. When was I ever going to be good enough as just me? Apparently not here either. Here I was trying to be a good leader, to open the youth ministry up to all kinds of youth, but I was being told I couldn't be my full authentic self.

I was crushed. How do I become less than myself to please the church? Why did I have to? I wasn't seen—or was I?

I wasn't secure enough in my voice or close enough to the pastor to stand up for myself. Keep the peace, Amy. Don't talk, don't trust, don't feel. They didn't see me. So, I held back my energy and passion and the church got a lesser version of me.

Being seen is important to every human being. It validates our humanity, our existence. Those who have a relationship with God are at a distinct advantage in seeing others, as we see through the lens of God. We have the "muscle" that helps us see others through that lens, if we exercise it daily.

FIVE

A DIFFERENT KINDA CHRISTIAN

Normal people keep the world going,
but those who dare to be different lead us into tomorrow.

KYRIE IRVING

One fall afternoon in Chicago, I was standing outside the Humboldt Park church where I was the youth pastor, welcoming guests to an event we were hosting. I had on jeans and a T-shirt that said "These ARE my church clothes." An older white lady approached me and asked if I attended this church.

"Yes, ma'am, I do," I politely said.

"And they let you wear that?" she asked in judgment.

"Absolutely!" I exclaimed.

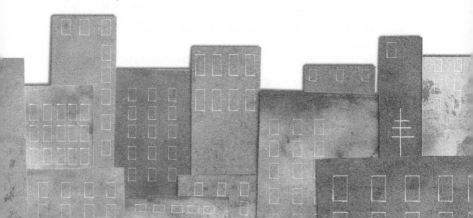

"Well, I would never," she said in disgust. "God doesn't like that."

"I think God loves simply that I'm here no matter what I'm wearing," I said. "I hope you enjoy the service today."

She walked off mumbling something under her breath as I welcomed the next guest. That became my favorite T-shirt to wear, especially in unexpected places.

I've never been one to fit in . . . and never really wanted to. I just wanted to be free to be me. I always knew I was different but didn't grasp the full meaning of that. I remember the D.A.R.E. (Drug Abuse Resistance Education) program's slogan, "Dare to be Different," and I wanted to be. I would scream it at the TV when the commercials came on. Looking back now, I am thankful that I was different, because in my adult years there would be many challenges due to being different that I would be prepared for.

HIP-HOP AND JESUS?

No matter, we still gon' kick it
And we ain't getting trippy,
No molly in my sippy
Ain't fighting nobody, ain't nobody set tripping.[1]

I had never experienced anything like it before: a church that looked, sounded, and acted like *me*. A hip-hop church. A church that had all elements of hip-hop honoring God.

Prolly think I'm rolling, I'm just high on the spirit bro
The only thing we popping is the truth, you don't hear
    me though[2]

It was Chicago's first hip-hop church with the intention of reaching a generation of young people through a culture that represented them. A church that was culturally relevant and had hundreds and hundreds of young people worshiping God to a hip-hop beat. It was taking the culture most of us grew up in and using it for God's glory. The sounds of bass line beats, the art of break dancers flipping and spinning on the stage, the eloquence of spoken word poetry, the DJ mixing sounds and songs, the emcees praising God with their lyrics, a screen full of messages written in graffiti fonts—and a pastor who embodied all of that with a preaching style that would lead many youth and young adults to Christ every single night. I felt like I was home.

This church gave me permission to fully be who I was during that season of my walk. I grew up hip-hop; I was still hip-hop. Yes, not many people were embracing it, but I found a family that understood it and embraced all of me along with it. Night after night, I would enter a crowded standing-room-only church preaching a gospel message of hope and love in a relevant fashion—and I loved it. Nothing about me was traditional, so why should my church be?

IT'S A GUY THING

After moving to North Carolina in 1982, I was bullied by Black girls throughout my teen and college life. I didn't understand why, but it was hurtful that I was bullied for something I couldn't control—the way I looked. As a result, I limited my female friendships and hung around with my first best friend (my brother) and his friends. I grew up around boys. I knew how to connect with them. I knew how to be friends with them without any further complications. They protected me and treated me like their sister. What I know about boys, I learned from them. So, it's no surprise that I do cross-gender mentoring—a big no-no in many denominations, and I get why. We have seen inappropriate relationships between adults and young people in the church for decades. It can be dangerous if not done right with accountability and boundaries.

During a conference where I was teaching on mentoring, I began to share that I do cross-gender mentoring and work mostly with young boys in gangs and prisons. An older African American male stood up and proceeded to tell me I was wrong and doing harm to those boys. This was nothing new, but something about his approach rose up another side of me. I was *not* backing down. I knew what God called me to, and this man was not going to change that.

"Sir," I said respectfully. "Where I live, there are too many gang members without mentors. Now I know I can't teach a boy how to be a man, but until the men in my community step up, I'm doing the work.

"If a kid is lying in the middle of the street bleeding out," I continued, "I'm not going to let him die because I'm a woman. I'm going to help that kid survive—and that's what I do every day. Just help them survive."

There may be an extra set of rules for those of us who mentor the opposite sex as safety precautions, and they are needed, but when you know what you are called to do, you move full steam ahead in that direction, even while taking precautions.

THAT KINDA CHRISTIAN

The first time I met sixteen-year-old Edgar, he walked into a conference room at a Christian Community Development Association (CCDA) conference where hip-hop music was playing and a loud woman was greeting everyone with a lot of energy (that lady was me). He was part of a ministry in Kansas City that ministered mostly to immigrant youth and families. His leader told him it didn't matter what topic she was teaching—they were going to her workshop. After the workshop was completed, Edgar came up to me and said he had never seen or heard anything like that before. I had the opportunity to meet with his group for dinner, and we all immediately clicked. A mentor relationship began quickly after that where I would visit Kansas City and they would visit Chicago.

During a visit to Kansas City, Edgar, his leader (and close friend of mine), Megan, and I went to a Bible study at a church member's home. Edgar seemed a little down but glad to be there. I pulled him aside and asked him what was wrong.

"Amy, I can never really be a Christian," he sadly said.

"Why do you believe that?" I asked.

"Because I can never be like *them*," he said.

"Like who?" I asked curiously.

"Them. White people. Megan and Tom and . . . them. White people," he said, exasperated.

"So what does being 'them' look like?"

"You know, always happy," he started. "Always so sure about God. Always nice and kind. Just always . . . perfect. I will never be able to be perfect, even with God."

I could feel his frustration and sadness, like a heavy weight on his shoulders.

"Then I met you," he continued. "And I didn't know you were a Christian." (Should I have been offended?) "I mean, you listened to hip-hop. You were having fun. You were more like me. I've never seen a Christian like you, only them . . . and I'm nothing like them."

He went on to explain he had never seen or met a Latino Christian, especially a man. The ministry he was part of had only white leaders: no one who looked like or could relate to him. He shared his love for them but also his frustration at a Christianity that seemed far beyond his reach.

"I am so happy you shared this with me," I exclaimed. "Because the enemy would love nothing more than for you to believe that lie. You are a unique individual, Edgar, and God doesn't want you to be like them. He wants you to be fully you."

We continued talking about God's desire for Edgar to be fully himself as a third culture teenager (fourth culture if you add his faith), a hip-hop lover, a first-generation Mexican American, and much more. We talked about how Jesus wasn't a white man but more like our skin color. We talked about what it means to be a man of God. We talked about how white evangelicals tend to worship the God of celebration, while churches of color connect with Jesus in his suffering. We talked and talked until Edgar felt free to experience God as Edgar. His goal wasn't to be "like" anyone other than himself and Jesus.

We opened the conversation to the group so they could fully understand where Edgar was in his journey, so that others could walk with him as he discovered who he was in Christ. After Edgar opened up, I had real conversations with the leadership and felt a shift in that ministry. Edgar created change just by simply asking to be seen.

We were created to be different. Individually unique in every way. We live in a world where being different is acceptable. It's our differences that bring value to the world. The battle comes in accepting our uniqueness in this world, including our flaws and imperfections. Being fully who you are is a gift to this world and can be used to make a great impact in the kingdom.

SEEING OTHERS

SIX

LETHAL ABSENCE OF HOPE

The absence of hope can rot a society from within.

BARACK OBAMA

Latisha walked around school unbathed, hair undone, teeth unbrushed. She didn't care and thought no one else did either. She rarely smiled, barely ever laughed. She was a young teen mother who'd been raped by her mother's boyfriend and become pregnant. She was forced by her mother to give birth to the child and held responsible for raising him. The look in her eyes was empty, almost lifeless. Her arms bore marks of self-harm. She had lost hope that life would get better.

One evening she called me, ready to end it all. She was severely depressed. I wasn't a counselor but I knew I had to get her

to a hospital. We walked through the experience together—long days, longer nights. After a month of intense treatment in the hospital, she was working toward healing and started smiling again. Hope was on the horizon.

Most of my youth make plans for their funerals, not their futures. You can ask them what their plan is for the next five years and they most likely will say, "To be alive"—and they aren't sure about that. But ask them about their funerals and they have an elaborate plan, or at least a semblance of what they want and don't want. The problem isn't that kids aren't scared enough; it's that they aren't hopeful enough.[1] Why do so many youth know what color casket they want but not what kind of job they desire? Father Greg Boyle of Homeboy Industries believes it's one thing: a lethal absence of hope.

You can drive through certain neighborhoods and tell the people there are living in hopelessness. What are signs that may indicate the absence of hope? Poor school systems, poverty, drug culture, addiction, trash everywhere, a culture of violence, and many more signs. Most of these problems are systemic, and in cities, they are most frequently found in communities of color, communities that lack resources invest in young people and build healthy, thriving neighborhoods.

> THE PROBLEM ISN'T THAT KIDS AREN'T SCARED ENOUGH; IT'S THAT THEY AREN'T HOPEFUL ENOUGH.

Hopelessness can look like a street corner infiltrated with drug dealers and drug users, a bridge where the homeless temporarily reside, an inmate in gen pop or solitary confinement, a sex worker being used for her body, a teenager contemplating suicide, a single mother who can't feed her kids. Hopelessness has many faces, but it can be met with the hope that is within us . . . the teachers, mentors, pastors, corner store clerks, and so on.

As Father Boyle shared on an episode of *Dr. Phil*, "The problem with many young people who get in trouble or join gangs is a lethal absence of hope. If someone can't imagine a future for himself, then his present isn't compelling. If his present doesn't compel him, then he doesn't care if he inflicts harm on others or ducks to get out of the way."[2] If there is no hope present, then what you do doesn't matter. Having hope changes what you do, what you believe, what you say. Hope changes how you see yourself and what you value.

"You can't scare a kid straight. You have to *care* a kid straight," continues Father Boyle.[3]

When my young people tell me they have no hope, I get it. Then I tell them I will hope for them until they can hope for themselves. We need to infuse kids with hope because we are called to be hope in hopeless situations.

INFUSING HOPE

How do we infuse hope into people who feel there is no hope? This has been a challenge for centuries. Even in the Bible we see many stories of hopelessness. Many issues today are systemic and require widespread advocacy and reform. But we can make an impact on individuals through our encouragement. There are a few ways I have seen hope blossom in young people using these strategies.

Expose them to new people, environments, and opportunities. Exposing people to new things expands their worldview and challenges their limited experiences. Letting them see a world outside their own creates hope. I am known for taking youth to Chick-fil-A and the beach/lake for the first time. You'd be amazed by the small things some young people have never been exposed to. What a great opportunity for us.

Surround them with a new community of mentors who can speak life to them. Most of my young people in prison realize their "boys" were not there for them when they got locked up. I often hear them say they need to be around positive people when they get home because that's who will keep them out of trouble. When I started a basketball team for youth on the block, my goal was to introduce them to positive male role models and expand their current circle. We can be that community that surrounds them.

Speak of hope often and share stories of overcoming hopelessness. Young people need to hear and see more about hope when what they see most often is stories of hopelessness. In prison, I seek instructors who have been in prison themselves and are living successful lives. Introducing young people to these stories of hope and success inspires and gives them hope.

RESTORING HOPE

Hope dealers aren't supposed to feel hopeless. But I have to admit I have felt exactly that at times, especially when I keep burying my young people over and over again. What do you do as a leader when your own hope is borderline? How do you renew hope when you're emotionally drained?

At the core, we lose hope when we take our eyes off of God, when we stop trusting him and we forget our place. Here are my tips for restoring hope in ourselves.

Know your role. Just a reminder. Where is the hope in that? This kind of hope requires you to trust that God loves you enough, loves that person enough, and knows what's best. The hope is that people will have a God experience that strengthens their hope, and this releases us from being God.

Remember we can't change or save anyone. It's not our re-sponsibility. Where is the hope in that? It releases the enormous weight of needing a positive outcome based on what we have done. God is the God of his people. He changes and molds the hearts of his people. All we are called to do is love them in the process.

> WE LOSE HOPE WHEN WE TAKE OUR EYES OFF OF GOD, WHEN WE STOP TRUSTING HIM AND WE FORGET OUR PLACE.

Get good at waiting. We tend to lose hope when we lose patience, which is really a trust issue. A good example is when I started to learn salsa dancing. The man is supposed to lead, and the woman follows (yep, you already see where I'm going with this). It's hard to dance well with a partner if you don't trust them. I used to be stiff and lead myself, and it was a train wreck—every time. I needed to be patient in where I was in the learning process, as well as where my partner was. There were many times I thought I was never going to be a good dancer, but I needed to be patient with myself. Where's the hope in that? It allows us not to get in God's way and mess things up. It also releases us from being God.

Remember we only get to see part of the picture. We tend to lose hope when we don't understand how all the pieces we see work together when the truth is we will never see all the intricate and strategic ways God makes a situation happen. And honestly, I think we would be overwhelmed if we knew and saw all the plans and details. When my niece died, I came to the conclusion that I don't have to like it, I don't have to understand it, but I do have to respect it because he is God. He knows all the details and reasons—even if he doesn't ever show me. I trust that God knows the plans he has for me (Jeremiah 29:11). Where's the hope in that? If we saw everything, then it would be about what we can do, not how God can show off. It also releases us from being God.

Ask what you are really putting your hope in. Are we putting our hope in our limited or incomplete abilities? Are we putting our hope in people? In things? We tend to transfer the hopelessness we feel about ourselves (limited abilities) into hopelessness in God, when the two are not even in the same room. Maybe we put too much hope in our obedience, too much hope in our programming, too much hope in past successes, and too much hope in the youth. The Word points us in the right direction: "And so, Lord, where do I put my hope? My only hope is in you" (Psalm 39:7 NLT). Where's the hope in that? It releases us from being God. Period.

SEVEN

THE BUSINESS OF SEEING OTHERS

God's purpose for man is to acquire a seeing
eye and an understanding heart.

RUMI

Rev. Raphael Warnock during his Senate election acceptance speech in December 2022 stated, "You cannot lead the people unless you love the people. You cannot love the people unless you know the people. And you cannot know the people unless you walk among the people. . . . You cannot serve me if you cannot see me."

Our business is seeing others, seeing them the way God sees them and letting them know they are seen and valued. People

are lonely, hurting, alone. No one should feel that way. But things get in the way of our ability to see. How can we see others when the way we see ourselves is skewed? How do we see others when our worldview is limited? And how does God really see his people?

Pastor John Perkins often says, "You don't give dignity; you affirm it." When we see people through God's eyes and hear their stories, we restore their dignity and help them flourish. When we embrace the humanity of others, we validate their existence and worth. Don't just see the person struggling with homelessness when you drive to the corner. Acknowledge them, speak to them, bless them—affirm their humanity.

> OUR BUSINESS IS SEEING OTHERS, SEEING THEM THE WAY GOD SEES THEM AND LETTING THEM KNOW THEY ARE SEEN AND VALUED.

One of my all-time favorite quotes is, "You can't judge a book by its cover, but you also can't judge it by its first chapter."[1] We tend to judge people on a surface level without truly getting to know their story. People have many chapters in their lives, and our young people have many chapters left to write. The power of story changes how we view people—if (and only if) we listen. Story matters only if people listen. Story can change our perception, which can create compassion and empathy, which ultimately results in action. In order to truly see others, we must give them the space and undivided attention to tell their stories. And beyond listening is validation. Validation shows support and recognition of one's journey. We do this through creating relationships of trust and authenticity, creating spaces, and being patient as one shares their heart, pain, and journey. Let the stories be told!

■ ■ ■

Derrick was one of those children who needed a lot of attention. He lost his mom to drugs and had a dad who worked all the time, barely there. When his dad was home, he was drinking and screaming at Derrick and his brothers. No matter how many A's he brought home from school, his dad never acknowledged his hard work. All he wanted was his dad's approval, to be seen— like the men on the block who wooed him and initiated him into the gang. When his dad found out he was a gang member, he beat Derrick to the point of putting him in the hospital.

"At least he sees me now," said Derrick with a faint, painful smile. "He now sees."

■ ■ ■

Perception is everything. Perception is the way you think about or understand someone or something. In the end (and the beginning), perception determines how you see and treat others. Let's look at how it works.

Perception starts with a foundation, a belief you were either taught or believed for yourself. For this lesson, we will use the belief that I was taught by my mother as an example: "Biracial people have the best of both worlds. If people have an issue with you being biracial, that's their problem." This is the foundation I was taught and is a value I have a strong belief in. Our foundational belief determines *what we think*. My thoughts are determined by what I believe. In turn, this also influences *what I say*.

For example, I have always heard (and been told) that biracial children are confused. When someone challenges me with

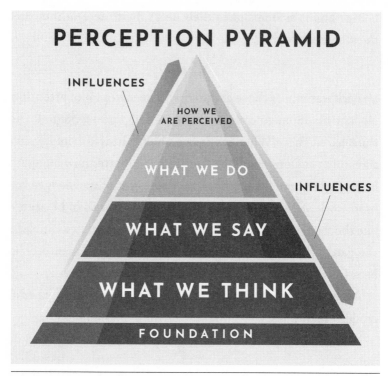

Figure 2. Perception pyramid

that foundational opinion, I respond to them based on what I believe and know to be true from my experience. What I say then determines *what I do*. I don't get mad, I don't fight, but I engage in conversation and use my words and experience to try to influence their foundational belief. All of these things will determine *how I am perceived* and, possibly, how others are perceived. But perception all starts with a foundational belief.

This is why story is so important. Story can change our perception of someone. I always say if you knew the stories of the youth I work with, you would understand why they end up in gangs and in prison. It's the stories that explain why people are the way they are and how they arrive in certain situations.

The problem with perception is that we take our own view as truth. Let's look at figure 3. Because of how things are arranged, our brain thinks we're seeing triangles.

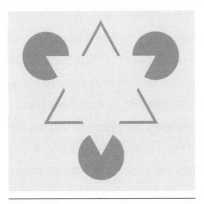

Figure 3. How many triangles are present in this image? Answer: There are no triangles. In reality, there are only three "V" shapes and three shapes that look like Pac-Man.

So what is reality? We have a lens of the world that has been shaped by our experiences, what we've been taught, and the input of others. As the quote goes, "we don't see things as they are. We see things as *we* are." For example, the way I see a gang member is going to be totally different from the view of someone whose child was killed by a gang member. We have a different lens, but which is truth? They both are. That's why story is important. We need more details, facts, statistics, and context to get a better understanding of why people are the way they are so we can be better ministers.

Perception can also be influenced by how we are feeling at any given moment. One moment I can feel joy watching a child laugh as she builds a sand castle, and the world is a good place. Then ten minutes later I can be irritated by that same child flinging sand in the wind that gets in my hair, and the world is annoying. Everything is the same but my feelings; my mind has changed my perspective.

If we are in the business of seeing others, we must be aware of what impacts our perception and how limited our lens is. We must ask questions, seeking not only to listen but to truly understand. This is why it is important to see how God views people. If we see through that lens, we can affirm the humanity and dignity of others.

■ ■ ■

I love the Madea movies. In *Madea's Family Reunion*, a memorable moment occurs when Madea says to her niece, "It ain't what people call you; it's what you answer to." This leads to an important question: Do you know who you are? Do you know *whose* you are? How you view yourself determines how you respond to people, but it also determines how you see others. We often hear that how we treat others is how we are actually being treated ourselves. But we should treat others the way we desire to be treated—with respect, dignity, and compassion. If we are not receiving this treatment, it's hard to treat others this way.

If young people in gangs or prisons see themselves as worthless and useless, how do you think they will see others? If someone is being abused, how do you think they feel about their own worth? How we see ourselves is directly related to how we accept and view others. The danger to this may be measuring our own worth by what others (whose worldview is forever changing) say and think. We can't depend on that.

This is why we must first see ourselves through the eyes of God. My favorite Scripture is Psalm 139, particularly these verses:

> For you created my inmost being;
>> you knit me together in my mother's womb.
> I praise you because I am fearfully and wonderfully made.
>> (Psalm 139:13-14 NIV)

If we can affirm our own worth and humanity, we can help others to do the same. How do we do this? By staying in the Word of God, praying constantly, and surrounding ourselves with a community where others are seeking to understand as well. Write it down. Post it all over the house. Seek God to get a closer, clearer, more accurate view of God's picture of you. I once heard that God's refrigerator is covered with pictures of you. I need that constant reminder.

■ ■ ■

Seeing others means we see them as they are, not how we want them to be. "Go and love someone exactly as they are. And then watch how quickly they transform into the greatest, truest version of themselves. When one feels seen and appreciated in their own essence, one is instantly empowered."[2] I have watched young people be one way with their boys, one way with their parents, and another way with me. I believe that's because I create safe spaces. The boys are more themselves when they are with me, because I allow them to fully be who they are in those moments—no pretenses, facades, or fake fronts. Do they know who they are? In most cases, no. Do they know they don't have to pretend with me? Absolutely, as the relationship develops. And all I do is love them as they are. I love this Max Lucado quote: "God loves you just the way you are, but he refuses to leave you there."[3] May we model that kind of relationship.

> **SEEING OTHERS MEANS WE SEE THEM AS THEY ARE, NOT HOW WE WANT THEM TO BE.**

■ ■ ■

Genesis 1:27 clearly tells us that "God created mankind in his own image, in the image of God he created them" (NIV). If he created you in his image, why would we look at others as less than? Because we're human and tend to forget God's love for all people. We see people and wonder, How could God love *that*? I've done it myself. But whether we see it or not, he does. God loves his people. His heart breaks often for those outside his will, those wreaking havoc on our world, those lost deep in sin, but his love for his people will always be. That is the base, the foundation we start with when viewing others—he loves us all and we are created in his image. From there we begin to individualize and add experience and story to our viewpoint, being careful to remember our own biases, pains, and experiences.

People tend to look down at others, especially those on the margins, but as Christians, that's not an option for us. I once heard a pastor say, "You cannot minister effectively to those you think less of." God defends the cause of the fatherless, widow, and orphan (Deuteronomy 14:28-29). We are to love the stranger and fear the Lord. As we do, we are reminded by apostle Paul, "I give each of you this warning: Don't think you are better than you really are. Be honest in your evaluation of yourselves, measuring yourselves by the faith God has given us" (Romans 12:3 NLT).

To see others, we must take the humble posture of a learner, someone with compassion, "a compassion that can stand in awe at what the poor have to carry rather than stand in judgment at how they carry it. No darkness to separate us. Only kinship."[4] To see others, we must remember we are in this thing called life together. We journey together, and we are made better because we do this together. God created us to long for kinship, to need kinship. Knowing kinship and togetherness creates change and healing. There are people praying for someone like you who will stop and see them the way God does. Let's create this kind of world.

EIGHT

THE PRIVILEGE OF PRESENCE

*And as we let our own light shine, we unconsciously give other
people permission to do the same. As we are liberated from
our own fear, our presence automatically liberates others.*

MARIANNE WILLIAMSON

I've never felt such deep, dark sadness in the air as I did the day
Jose was killed in a gang brawl. I picked up his younger brother
Nick from the police station, and we drove thirty minutes in
complete silence, me reaching over to offer gentle touches on his
shoulder every so often to try to console this inconsolable young
man. He had lost his mother to cancer only two days before.

We pulled up on Beach Avenue and there were fifty to seventy-
five people standing around Jose's house, anxiously waiting

for Nick. Many of Jose's family lived on this block, and if you grew up with him on Beach, you were considered family. There were posters of Jose and his mom, lit candles and memorabilia lovingly placed along the fence around the house. The air was cloudy from all the kush being smoked. I could barely breathe. The mood was grim, hopeless, sad, and now and then, you would hear a scream of pain coming from someone who couldn't believe Jose was gone. I spent hours walking around hugging, crying, and listening to every person who needed someone to talk to, knowing there were no words to bring comfort.

I saw some of my young people sitting on the stoop across from Jose's house. As I made my way over, the kush grew stronger and stronger. Since I have never smoked in my life, my lungs are often irritated by smoke, but today I didn't care. I knew my clothes, my hair, and my car would all smell like weed by the time this was over, and my lungs would feel like I smoked a blunt myself. But today I didn't care. A cop I knew who was patrolling the street (protocol in Chicago when a gang member is killed) drove by and nodded at me, knowing today was not the day to have a conversation. I needed to be with my boyz.

"Hey, Miss Amy," they all said sadly as I hugged them hello. There was a new kid there I had never met. We'll call him Marcos.

I sat between Marcos and Angelito, Jose's close cousin who had lost his own brother to gun violence two years prior. I rubbed Angelito's back for comfort. Everyone was super high, eyes pretty much shut, numbing the pain they couldn't bear to feel.

"You smoke? You want some?" asked Marcos as he held the blunt up in the air, offering it to me.

"Naw, she don't smoke, man!" exclaimed Angelito. "You know she a pastor. Get that out of her face!"

Everyone laughed loudly and called Marcos some hood names I can't mention here.

"For real! A pastor?" Marcos shouted as he started choking and coughing.

"Yup, used to be a youth pastor," I said proudly. "Now I'm the youth pastor of da block."

"I gotta write this down," exclaimed Marcos. "I can't believe dis."

"Believe what?" I asked.

"I can't believe I am smoking with a pastor," he said in awe as he took another hit of his blunt.

"Hold up now," I warned. "You ain't smoking *with* a pastor. You're smoking *beside* one. There's a difference. I don't roll like that, homie!"

The whole stoop busted out laughing as they playfully punched Marcos.

"But why you out here hanging with us?" Marcos said.

"Why wouldn't I be here?" I asked. "Jose and Nick are my boyz. I love them. Y'all are too! I need to be here with y'all."

"Amy is the real deal, man," Angelito said as he side-hugged me. "She's always around checking on us, doing things for us, and she loves us just as we are without trying to change us. She's the real deal."

I reached over and hugged Angelito back with a huge smile on my face. "Awww, Lito. That means a lot."

"You mean a lot to us, Miss Amy," Angelito declared.

"I still can't believe it," repeated Marcos he took another hit and blew it in the air toward my face.

"I get that," I said. "But you ain't gotta blow it in my face."

"My bad. It's the wind." Marcos said, as we all laughed again.

"I appreciate the love, though," I said, understanding that sharing a blunt is a sign of respect and caring.

An hour or so later I ran into Marcos again, and he stopped me to ask me something he had been thinking about since our encounter.

"Miss Amy, I ain't never seen no pastor out here on Beach," he said. "But fo real. Why would you come here?"

"Well for one, I moved here and live a couple streets over, so this is my block too. Y'all are my people." I started. "But mostly because I hate how this world treats y'all and I just want you to know that someone cares and that God is madly in love with you."

"Man, I got mad respect for you," he said as he reached out for a hug.

We then talked about the hood, Jose, and God. Three of my favorite things.

Presence is everything, but consistency of presence is more than that. Too often we set boundaries around places we as Christians should or shouldn't be seen or should or shouldn't go. We set these boundaries out of fear. When I share a story like the one above, the first reaction I get is usually the same as the kids': "What are you doing there with all that weed and liquor around?"

My answer: "Where else would Jesus be?"

Jesus would not have been sitting in a comfy church waiting for these young kids to come to him. He wouldn't wait until the funeral to be with them in their grief. He would be in the thick of it like he was with the Samaritan woman at the well. Jesus went *to* the man at the pool on the Sabbath. Jesus went *to* the blind man in Galilee. Jesus went *to* Lazarus in Judea, knowing the Jews there wanted him dead. He even went *to* Hades for us.

A good pastor friend of mine once shared a conversation he had with a gang leader. The gang leader told him they were both in the same business: the business of recruiting people. But he said there was one difference: "When a kid goes to the corner store, he sees me. When he goes to school, he walks right by me. When he's out playing with his friends, I am right there. When they need me, they know where I am. But when they need *you*, they have to come find you."

Many churches have an open-door policy, but the question is, who's actually walking through your doors? Are you out in the community enough that if someone had a real need, they would know where to find you? Is your presence known? Or is it only members of the church who have that access to you?

People on my block always knew they would see me at some point in the week, just stopping by to check on them or simply to hang out. I was their resource advocate and the first person they came to when they needed prayer. They had expectations. They knew they could count on this crazy lady in her green Acura with the dented door driving through the block to say hello. We were in this together.

A friend once said to me, "The whole world will decide who Jesus is by who we are." Marcos had already decided what a pastor was. Maybe that changed on this day. We have the responsibility to see the image of God in everyone we meet. It's a muscle we must work daily. That day I saw God everywhere, in every grieving soul. And I pray they saw God present with them in every hug or smile I shared.

> WE HAVE THE RESPONSIBILITY TO SEE THE IMAGE OF GOD IN EVERYONE WE MEET. IT'S A MUSCLE WE MUST WORK DAILY.

Not everyone is called to move into a gang neighborhood, but you are called to go somewhere. Where is that place, and when was the last time you were there? Where are people in your community who need someone who's not afraid to be with them as they are, where they are? No judgment, just love.

When people know I intentionally moved into a gang neighborhood, they often ask me, "But weren't you scared?" Truth is, I was never scared. For me, it's hard to be scared of young people you have a relationship with. When God called me to this work, it brought more peace than fear. Knowing he called me to this neighborhood gave me confidence to do what he was asking me to do. If he had called me to live with those he wanted me to serve, he had to have my back—and that's what I was counting on.

You can't minister or serve those you fear. If you do, they're just projects, clients, not real people with real needs, real desires, real lives. We fear what we do not know. There are times when fear is real and valid. There are also times when we must push through the fear, take the time to get to know the stories of others, and move to relationship.

What does it mean to "develop community" with others? For some of us, it's moving onto the block, hanging out on that corner, heading into that community. When I had that conversation with God about moving into a gang neighborhood, one of my responses was, "But Lord, I can do ministry with youth in gangs without *living* among them."

I immediately heard him say, "True, but these youth? They need you there."

The fact is, for me to serve these young people, they needed my consistent presence. They needed to see I was committed. They needed to see I was invested in them and the block. I considered this a sacred holy space to walk with them in. Walt Whitman said, "We convince with our presence." Moving into the community created a new relationship. It went from *they* and *them* to *we* and *us*. Now when you throw trash on the ground on my block, I care because this is my block too. I can advocate for change in the neighborhood.

But one thing to note here: I didn't come in marching around like I owned the block. They had been there long before me, some for generations. I was the newcomer and I needed to act accordingly. I was not the savior of the block. I needed them to teach me the ins and outs, the history, the dos and don'ts. I needed to find my place, slowly but surely letting them know I was here for the long haul. They taught me, and I learned. We are now in this together.

One of the many privileges of being a woman living in the neighborhood is that I can go places most men can't. I have observed on numerous occasions an unknown male coming through the block generating tension, apprehension, and even fear. Most of the youth believe outsiders are undercover cops. They even thought I might be one, but my consistency and presence proved them wrong. I can walk the block with barely any issues other than the regular catcalls (not from my youth).

As much as these young men needed male mentors, female mentors played a vital role in their lives. I became the mom, the auntie, the big sis. They would cry with me when no one was around. They would hug me when others got a fist bump. They felt safe driving with me. And much more. God uses my woman-hood as a way to impact lives. They invited me into spaces they normally wouldn't invite a man into. To this day, I am humbled by that.

For those not called to move into the places they serve, they still have the responsibility to be present in those spaces. If you worship in the city but live in the suburbs, how are you making sure your presence in the city is impactful? Is your church just a building in the neighborhood, or is its presence felt? If your church shut down right now, would the community feel it? The church has the power to transform neighborhoods through its presence. Presence and consistency are the keys to creating authentic relationships. How can the church advocate on behalf of the neighborhood if they're not seen as a presence?

Bryan Stevenson says it wonderfully when he states, "Current solutions don't work because they haven't been shaped by the insights and knowledge that come from proximity and from the communities involved. We need to get close enough to wrap our arms around [those who suffer] and affirm their humanity."[1] We can't solve problems from a distance. Presence says I see you. I see your need and we're in this together. Learn the value of your presence. In many communities, the church has done this. What about yours?

> PRESENCE AND CONSISTENCY ARE THE KEYS TO CREATING AUTHENTIC RELATIONSHIPS.

PEOPLE ARE NOT PROJECTS

People are not projects to be fixed.
 Period.

IT'S NOT ABOUT FIXING PEOPLE

Don't confuse getting noticed with being seen.

Tanya Geisler

Did I get the point across in the last chapter? Too often in ministry, we take the stance that once we become Christians, we are the experts in healing. We look at others like we own the cure to everyone's instant healing. And somehow, we begin to make people into projects we are called to "fix." That's what I was taught by the first church I joined. Though Jesus is a cure, he also uses many tools for us to get to the place of complete healing—and everyone heals differently, on different timelines, from different traumas and hurts. Unless your profession is

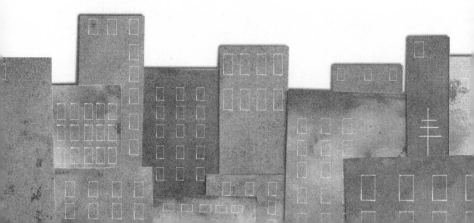

medicine or mental health, your job is not to "fix" people—and even they can only do so much. Let's dig deeper.

■ ▪ ■

Trey and I, along with a couple of other youth, were hanging out on the block on a hot summer afternoon having a great time. As I walked Trey back home, we ended up talking about his brother.

"Amy, I'm doing real good," he said proudly. "My brother needs help. You can go hang out with him now. I'm good."

I felt a lump in my throat and a dagger in my heart. Did Trey think I was out here helping youth just when they were in trouble or down and out? Did he think he was a project for me?

After explaining to him that's not what I was on, I went home and cried. I didn't really know what to say, but I felt horrible that somehow I had communicated to him that I was better, I knew better, and I was the answer to his life problems. All I wanted was to help and point him to God, but in that small exchange, I realized he saw me as the lady who moved into the hood to help youth as her mission. Yes, that was true—to an extent—but I didn't want it to be at the expense of people feeling they needed to change to what I thought was in their best interest. That meant I took the lead role, was the divine guide—the know-it-all. The truth was, I had no idea what was best for Trey or his brother, but God did. I am thankful for that exchange because it opened my eyes and changed my ministry. Thanks, Trey!

■ ▪ ■

This concept cannot be more clearly described than by Bob Lupton in *Theirs Is the Kingdom: Celebrating the Gospel in Urban America*:

When my goal is to change people, I subtly communicate there's something wrong with you; I'm okay. You are ignorant; I'm enlightened. You are wrong; I am right. If our relationship is defined as healer to patient, I must remain strong and you must remain sick for our interaction to continue. People don't go to doctors when they are well.

The process of "curing," then, cannot serve long as the basis for a relationship that is life-producing for both parties. Small wonder that we who have come to "save" the poor find it difficult to enter into true community with those we think are needy.[1]

What we are seeking with others as we walk with them is kinship, not dictatorship. Kinship is a feeling of being close or similar to other people. It is also a familial relationship. Though we are not literally family, we strive to become a close community with those we serve. As Father Greg Boyle states, "Kinship—not serving the other, but being one with the other. Jesus was not 'a man for others'; he was one with them. There is a world of difference in that."[2] Being with the other. Not better than. Not less than. But *with*.

Lupton mentions, "If our relationship is defined as healer to patient, I must remain strong and you must remain sick for our interaction to continue."[3] I don't want my youth to be sick. I want them healed! But understanding

> "KINSHIP—NOT SERVING THE OTHER, BUT BEING ONE WITH THE OTHER. JESUS WAS NOT 'A MAN FOR OTHERS'; HE WAS ONE WITH THEM."
> Gregory Boyle

this concept changes the hierarchy of relationship. I am no longer the leader. They aren't the followers. We are in this together. We teach each other. We both contribute to the relationship. Kinship.

For me, the hardest part about seeing people has been realizing that until someone wants to change, there is nothing you can do for them but be consistently present and pray. For someone like me who likes to be in control, it's hard to "let go" until someone needs you. One of my youth who was locked up introduced me to his friend in prison, thinking he desired mentorship and help when he was released. Marc was a well-known gang member in Little Village and had already served five years when I was introduced to him via the phone. We developed a mentor-mentee relationship over the phone and talked often. As I always do, I asked him what he wanted to do when he came home. (Ministry tip: Always make a plan before they come home.) He shared the basic answer all returning citizens say: a job. He further said he wanted to get into a music studio, be a better dad, and one day walk away from the life. He was honest with me that he wasn't sure he was ready, but I hoped he would be once I hooked him up with resources, other mentors, and a steady job.

I got the call while I was at a conference that he had been released and needed a ride. I left the conference and drove two hours to pick him up at the bus station where he was dropped off. As I pulled up to the entrance, I could tell he was nervous. We had never met in person, and his insecurities were overtaking him. I jumped out of the car and gave him a huge hug to break the ice. It probably freaked him out, but I'm a hugger. What can I say? He smiled and hugged me back.

Once we were in the car, I did everything I could to make him feel welcome and less anxious. Coming home from prison can create a lot of social anxiety, and I wanted him to feel comfortable being uncomfortable. We went to dinner at Applebee's for his first real meal in six years. He was a bit overwhelmed with the menu choices. After years of having no choices in prison, it can be a challenge to go to a restaurant, a grocery store, or even Subway with all those choices! I selected two items for him to choose from and the anxiety was lessened. We enjoyed our meal, though all he did was flirt with every female we came across. Yup, that was Marc for you. It was great finally being together in person.

Those first few weeks he was on home confinement. I called every day to check on him. His parole officer gave him movement (permission to leave home for an allotted time and specific location) when he was with me. I would pick him up to do basic things. I had a job ready for him, a free studio where he could do his music, a male mentor to connect with, a free car (that needed a little work), and a church to attend. I was ready.

He wasn't.

He ghosted me for a while and we lost contact. He stopped going to the job. Only went to the studio twice. Never connected with his mentor. Didn't take the car. Never went to church.

He wasn't ready.

Did it hurt? Yes! I busted my butt for him only to be left in the wind. I believed in him. The problem was he didn't believe in himself. It was too much, too fast . . . and his heart was still in the streets. A kid will never leave the streets until his heart leaves it first.

Months later, Marc was rearrested for a gruesome crime he didn't commit. (This case was dropped, but others remain.) He remembered my number and called me from lockup. Everyone told me to forget him and move on. I wanted to, but something in me just couldn't. He didn't have anyone, and he still needed a mentor. Our first phone call was awkward. I was still hurt, but I couldn't give up on him. I had a come-to-Jesus talk with him, set my boundaries, and guarded my heart. He was apologetic, but I needed action behind his words. In the same turn, I apologized for not recognizing he wasn't ready for all that change and was sorry if I pushed it on him. He was taken aback that I was apologizing, but it softened the awkwardness and released him from some of the burden.

To this day we talk often as we await his coming home. He may come soon. He may get a very long sentence. Maybe he's ready? Maybe he's not. He says he is this time, but I recognize that only Marc can be the hero of his story. I can provide resources and friendship, but he has to lead the charge . . . and when he's ready, I will be too.

You know you're treating people like projects when you need to keep them to yourself. You want to be the hero in their lives and take credit for their "turnaround." That used to be me, but God showed me.

I was blessed to know a young gang member, Joshua, who had a ton of questions about God. He was always challenging the status quo, and I loved that. We would spend hours talking about the deep things of God and my dysfunctional Christian family. I had introduced him to a male friend of mine, Miguel, and they would go at it for hours too. One day I invited Joshua to the hip-hop church to experience something different. While we were there, we ran into Miguel, and he sat with us. When the preacher asked if anyone needed prayer, Joshua looked at Miguel and asked him to go up with him.

I was crushed! I was jealous. I had known him longer! He was my kid! I had poured years into him, and he asked *Miguel*? God humbled me instantly. *He's mine, not yours. He needs you both.* I needed to surrender my will (and ego) and see how I was to *fit* into the plan God had for Joshua.

As people who serve others, we have to learn to release the stranglehold we have on individuals. Sometimes we hold them so close we choke them. They can't breathe. They say it takes a village to raise a kid. I say it takes a kingdom these days. We have to surround our young people with as many mentors, pastors, teachers, and community advocates as we can. They need to know and expand their social circles to include positive people who will not only love them but challenge them. It is our responsibility to open that space for them. I want all my boys to know as many positive men as I can introduce them to and hope some of them will click.

Too often we believe that God has "ordained" us to be the superhero in a person's life. We think we have all the wisdom, the programs, the resources, and the ability to change the heart and life of a person. But the truth is that all we can offer them is an uncompromising and unrelenting love that pursues them, unmovable support, and a joyous introduction to the one and only God who has the power to change their heart. . . and their life.

We must work on trusting that God is involved, he is aware of what is going on, he knows what will happen, and he (along with the Son and the Holy Spirit) is responsible for drawing the heart of men and women to a personal, intimate relationship with himself. God loves them more than we ever could.

I am not an expert on trauma, but I do know that every single one of the youth I have been blessed to serve has experienced life-altering trauma in their life as a child, ranging from abuse, homelessness, and sexual molestation to illness, bad divorces, bullying, and much more. Childhood trauma has adverse effects on adulthood and plays a huge part in teenage decisions. Many who've experienced trauma face PTSD with no treatment, counseling, or medication to help them through the darkness. They live with the trauma and try to survive it, carry it, and navigate through it.

In *Restoring the Shattered Self: A Christian Counselor's Guide to Complex Trauma*, trauma counselor Heather Gingrich shares that most people assume negative events at a young age do not affect the development or resilience of that child. They assume kids will be able to bounce back easily. "In fact, the opposite is true," she writes. "The younger the child, the greater the impact a potentially traumatic event often has, both in terms of neurobiology and psychology."[4] When working with high-risk youth or others, we cannot ignore the trauma they have encountered at a young age. We cannot ignore how much it affects where they are today in their lives and the choices they make.

As we examine the lives of others (or ourselves), we recognize that defensive responses differ for each individual: fight, flight, freeze, or fawn. As WebMD describes it, "The fight response is your body's way of facing any perceived threat aggressively. Flight means your body urges you to run from danger. Freeze is your body's inability to move or act against a threat. Fawn is your body's stress response to try to please someone to avoid conflict. The goal of the fight, flight, freeze, and fawn response is to decrease, end, or evade danger and return to a calm, relaxed state."[5] This means people can encounter the same event but be triggered and respond differently. "The particular defense response that is triggered at any given point in time depends both on the particulars of the specific situation and on past behavior and personal characteristics of the individual."[6]

Gingrich uses a car accident as an example—one that truly resonates with me. I was rear-ended once at a complete stop near a train track, and my response was to freeze. Others may have jumped right out of the car and angrily yelled at the driver, while others may have fought off any help offered to them. After my experience, I had PTSD for over a year. Anytime someone would drive up behind me or come close to my bumper, I would freeze and tense up (and sometimes cry). My body took on the trauma. The body remembers. I had to go to the chiropractor, who took months to get my muscles to finally relax. When I get in a car with someone else, my body tightens up for the entire ride. That trauma affected every area of my life, down to whether I would go hang out with friends because I would have to drive.

Among gang members and those who are incarcerated, trauma is as common as acne on a teenager's face. Every young person I have encountered has a story of deep trauma that has led them to this place in their lives. "Many are traumatic stress survivors," shares R. Dandridge Collins in *The Trauma Zone: Trusting God for Emotional Healing*. "Most, like brave soldiers, carried on with their lives until new demands brought the old wounds storming back to the surface."[7] I could tell you stories upon stories and you would understand how these individuals ended up where they did—in gangs, in prison—and you wouldn't blame them one bit. And being in gangs and in prison causes more trauma to the already traumatized.

Gangs appeal to traumatized youth. According to the National Child Traumatic Stress Network:

> A high number of delinquent and gang-involved youth have experienced abuse, neglect, maltreatment, as well as exposure to domestic and community violence. Exposure to community violence has been specifically shown to increase the risk of gang involvement. Incarcerated youth who profess gang involvement have been exposed to more violence and more severe violence than their peers who are not affiliated with gangs. Early childhood trauma, particularly abuse and neglect, is common among gang-involved youth.[8]

We also have to acknowledge that not everyone acknowledges their trauma or wants to be saved from it. Some individuals' whole identity is wrapped up in their trauma story, and healing can be scary. Many have no idea who they are outside of trauma, and that unknown can be more terrifying than staying in their comfort zone. I know a lady whose son was murdered over twenty years ago, and to this day her whole identity is her pain and loss. She cannot move past her trauma because she has created a world and reputation around it. There has been very little healing or forgiveness. Her trauma is her identity.

One thing to note here is that if you are not a professional, offering to counsel the traumatized is not the answer. You can offer support and connect people with resources to help them heal; I have referred many youth to both outpatient and inpatient treatment. I drive them there, visit, help cover costs, and so on. But I know my lane. And we don't want to do more damage if we're not equipped to professionally treat them.

As I write this, I am in Puerto Rico in the middle of a tropical storm. I sit and watch the ocean waves peak and roar. I see the palm trees bending back and forth trying to stay rooted in the soaked ground. I see the wind furiously blowing the red flags on the beach warning people this is not the time to go for a swim (but surfers don't care). I'm answering text messages from people checking on me to be sure I am safe.

I am reminded of the storms my young people go through daily, trying to stay grounded and rooted. Their insides are yelling to be loosed and freed. The red flags of rage are warning them to stay calm, that this is not the time to act out, yet they do anyway. I check on them to be sure they are safe. As this island is in a tumultuous state, so are many of my young people. Struggling, fighting, surviving. We want to be a safe harbor for them as they navigate the storm, pointing them to one famous for calming storms.

ELEVEN

OUTREACH IS A LIFESTYLE, NOT AN EVENT

We remember the people who saw us when
we couldn't really see ourselves.

JULIE WOLCOTT-HAIMS

One day I was hanging out on the doorstep of a well-known gang leader. I asked him about his perception of the church and the outreach events a lot of churches host during the summer months.

"So, how do you feel about those kind of block party outreaches?" I asked.

"Y'all can do as many of those that you want," he replied, "but it doesn't make that much of a difference."

"It doesn't?" I questioned, wanting to know more.

"If y'all come out and cook hot dogs and food, we'll eat it," he shared. "You play your music, we'll listen. Bring your basketball hoops and bouncy houses, we'll play. But other than that, we don't want to hear about your Jesus because we know you're not coming back until next year."

Not that I agree one hundred percent with him about the effectiveness of outreaches, but I have asked many of my gang-involved youth the same question, and they shared the same sentiment. And I completely understand why. My friend Ray Nelson says, "Community-day events must evolve into community-year presence." We come, we play, we leave. How is that effective?

When churches and organizations do outreach events that truly connect with the community, it's all about consistency and presence. They move beyond the "drive-by" event and plan multiple events in the same location, spend time with the residents, and connect them to resources. A great example is Chicago's Mothers Against Senseless Killings, a community of moms who take over corners with their presence, reducing crime and ending gun violence in those areas. I've seen a few churches that are consistently on the streets, connecting with community members, providing resources, and being present. It can be done.

Yes, it can be unsettling and scary to hang around outside on a beautiful day in Chicago with a young person connected to a gang. But the thing that's most unsettling and scary is how these young people, due to their choices and associations, have to spend their life watching their backs and always looking around. It's hard to have a good conversation outside because the focus is never fully yours. But we can pray for these young people who have no choice but to always watch their back.

What exactly is Christian outreach? Is it an event? Is it a project? How can we have a true impact on those in our communities in our efforts to reach out? I define outreach as the privileged opportunity to introduce Jesus Christ, intentionally demonstrate his love, and passionately share the message of hope to people who have not heard of the good news . . . but with a holistic approach. We don't need to bring people to Christ. We need to bring Christ to them.

> OUTREACH IS THE PRIVILEGED OPPORTUNITY TO INTRODUCE JESUS CHRIST, INTENTIONALLY DEMONSTRATE HIS LOVE, AND PASSIONATELY SHARE THE MESSAGE OF HOPE.

Many churches choose to use events as their primary approach to outreach, but my question is, what is your ultimate goal? Is it a means to introduce your church, grow church membership, and hand out bookbags? All of these may be beneficial and necessary. But I truly believe outreach is a lifestyle, not an event. Outreach is about the relationships you build that help people see the God we serve who loves them deeply.

TURNED OFF

Many of the young people I serve have been turned off *and* turned away by the church. Churches often take a "come to us" stance but have a "closed-door policy" for anyone who does not fit their set standards. These standards may include:

- Need to wear a suit and tie (many youth can't afford one and have no real need for one).
- No sagging or baggy pants (sure, this is cultural, but maybe they don't own a belt. Did you ask?).
- No cursing (if you can't be around cursing, this outreach work may not be for you).

About that last point: It may sound violent to your ears, but you will hear a lot of cursing when working with high-risk youth. Most will try not to curse in church or around Christians—many won't—but if they slip and curse, find a way to nonjudgmentally ask them to be more aware of their words in the church. Many of those who don't know or understand church culture may come from a family of cursers. That's all they hear. They don't even know they are cursing. This is not a deal breaker, but we tend to judge those who curse as if they had committed the greatest sin. Have some patience with youth who don't get church culture.

What's more, we often lay out salvation too systematically—you must do this, then that, then roll around three times in the mud, then sing for twelve hours, then . . . then . . . then. We have made salvation complicated, when the Bible simply says in Romans 10:9, "If you confess with your mouth that Jesus is Lord and believe in your heart that God raised him from the dead, you will be saved." Our youth need to connect with the simplicity of Jesus' love and humanity. Many of our methods are turnoffs because they require steps these youth don't understand.

I was standing on the block with the fellas early one hot summer evening when a white van with tinted windows pulled up. The van had a local church logo painted on the sides. Two white men jumped out and said they were from a local church and wanted to invite the young people to join them for a fun evening at church with lots of food and prizes. They had been driving around the block picking up youth. Some agreed and immediately jumped in, while others needed to get permission to go. I was in shock! I had never seen this before, but some of the older men on the block shared that this had happened before.

The next day I hunted down some of the youth to ask them what happened. They said they played games all night, ate pizza and drank 7-Up, and got a bunch of prizes. I asked if the organizers said anything about God.

"Yes," said Jesse. "I gave my life to Christ."

"That's amazing," I said excitedly. "Do you know what that means exactly?"

"Not really," he said, "but everyone was doing it."

I was angry. I was angry for many reasons, but I decided to wait for a bit to see what would happen next. I waited a week. I waited another week. I decided to ask Jesse a question.

"Jesse, have you heard from or seen any of those people from that church again?"

"Nope," he said casually.

My anger grew into a rage. I didn't know why I was feeling this way at first, but then I realized—you're playing with my babies. Taking them out of their community (communicating that God is not there) and bringing them to a whole other community instead of partnering with nearby churches to host the event.

I prayed and calmed down and called the church. I left several messages until the youth pastor finally called me back. We had quite the conversation, but I felt a deep need to protect my youth from this church, which appeared to be concerned only about event and salvation numbers rather than the hearts and lives

of these young people. We discussed the importance of neighborhood partnerships and the dangers of what they were doing.
They were causing more harm than healing for my youth on the
block. I had conversations with the youth, and many were disap-
pointed that they never saw the van come back. When our youth
are already dealing with abandonment issues, this can damage
the work the church is trying to do as a whole.

The church van never came back. I think I'm still mad.

A BURDEN FOR OUTREACH

Before you jump in and do this thing called outreach, I truly believe you must have a nagging, irritating burden that won't let
up—a passion for reaching young people. I have a few sugges-
tions that helped me build the relationships I needed to share
the love and hope of Jesus on fertile soil:

Change the way you view an unbelieving teen. The way you
view a teenager says a lot about how you view the world. Many
see teens as problem children—rebellious, troublemakers, lazy,
and so on. We tend not to see them as the strong, powerful,
talented, energetic people they are—people capable of changing
the world. A breath of fresh air. Changing the way you see a
teenager changes how you minister to them.

Watch your "language." Why do we use church language to
communicate with those who don't know it? "Christianese" is
the language of the saved, not the language of the world. In order
to communicate effectively, we must keep our Christianese to a
minimum until we begin discipling them on the vocabulary. And
please don't call them "unchurched." The last thing I am trying
to do is "church" a kid (I'm trying to get unchurched myself).
Let's focus on the relationship with God.

Don't focus on behavior. We are not in the business of behavior modification—the Holy Spirit does that. We are to focus on introducing people to the God of transformation. If I see the same gang member on the block always smoking weed, I'm not going to tell him to stop. That is not my focus. We may have conversations about it, but if that's my focus then I've lost him already. I will be seen as that judgy Christian—what a turnoff. Why would he want to be around me? I'll let God convict his heart. That's not my job.

Change the way you see yourself. We've talked about this in previous chapters. Know your role and remember, you are not the hero of their story, they are. Let God be God in their lives.

We have all seen large outreach events where many give their lives to Jesus. This is always a beautiful thing to witness, always brings me to tears, but I often wonder what happens to those who didn't make a commitment. Those who may have questions but won't step through the church doors. At outreach events, we often focus on the ones who made the decision to accept Christ, but what about those who didn't? Did we lose them? How can we change our events to focus on both?

All my boys on the block loved basketball—and smoking weed—but I learned early on that basketball was what God gave me to connect with them. I spent weeks researching and reaching out to churches about their gyms, asking if I could use them for my boys when they were empty. One pastor welcomed the opportunity, but unbeknownst to me he had an agenda. They could use the gym only if they sat (every time) and heard the message of Christ. That wasn't my strategy. My goal was to get youth off the streets, keep them safe, and build relationships with them—not force-feed God. The youth were not having it either.

I found another youth pastor at a large church who understood my purpose and was open to just letting youth play basketball. They even offered to help me pick up youth with vans!

One weekend we planned a two-day basketball program. We picked up a few of my youth by driving around the block on Saturday night (we even brought younger kids to play board games). They had a blast! And they went back that evening to tell others about it.

Sunday came around and I told everyone to be on the corner of Beach and Spaulding. When I arrived, there were over twenty young people all wanting to play basketball. I was excited! I had to call the pastor and tell him to bring two vans. As we were waiting for the vans, the police pulled up. We knew what was up. Someone had called the cops thinking something fishy going on.

Officer M. saw me and asked me what was going on as the vans pulled up. I explained what we were doing.

"No one has ever done anything like this for the youth here," he said. "This is kind of amazing, actually. Thank you. The streets will be safer tonight."

As a result of this weekend, I found a Christian basketball league and formed a team of youth from the block to participate. We called ourselves the Humboldt Park Playerz. I pray it was an impactful, fun experience for them.

FOR MEMBERS ONLY

My very small block had a total of five churches, and I never saw any of them walking the block or going door to door. One church had a gentle, kind man who stood on the corner every day for a few hours just to speak to everyone. We had lots of good conversations, and the kids knew who he was.

I attempted to reach out to every church's youth pastor with no success. One Spanish-speaking church in particular had a parking lot, a rare thing to see in the Chicago neighborhoods. I noticed they only used the parking lot on Sunday mornings and Wednesday evenings. What a great opportunity to use it for something else, like basketball, volleyball, and soccer! I went by the church, but there was no name on the building and no one inside. I called and left several messages for the youth pastor, even the senior pastor. I wanted to partner up and see how we could reach the youth on the block. Nada.

I decided to go by the church on a Wednesday before their Bible study to try to catch someone. I met a nice young lady but she didn't speak English. I grabbed one of my youth standing on the corner to translate. She wasn't interested in my proposal and said we couldn't use the parking lot. It was for church members only. I was heartbroken and mad.

This church had an incredible opportunity to reach its community but chose to serve only those who walked through its doors. As the church, we must take advantage of what God has given us to steward to have the most impact as possible. We must reach beyond the church walls. There are people—families, neighborhoods, and communities—who desperately need the hope of God, and we are called to offer that. We must meet people where they are at and then take them further.

> THERE ARE PEOPLE WHO DESPERATELY NEED THE HOPE OF GOD, AND WE ARE CALLED TO OFFER THAT.

I attended an event one Friday afternoon. After the event I noticed there were leftover sandwiches. I asked if I could have them, and the organizers were glad they didn't have to throw them away. So I rolled up on the block and found a group of my boys standing around smoking weed.

"Anyone hungry?" I yelled.

They all ran over and I proceeded to hand out the sandwiches. Kids came from their porches and their houses to grab a sandwich. We all hung around. Somehow two of the kids started a rap battle. I pulled out my phone where I had about twenty-five instrumental beats and started playing it out loud. People were jumping in the cipher rhyming. Should I? Could I? Did I? Yes. Yes, I did. I jumped in with a sweet rhyme of my own. They were shocked and started screaming and hugging me. After that, I was MC Pastora.

Sometimes outreach is as simple as a sandwich and a rhyme.

Our hope and promise:

> I will lead the blind
>   in a way they do not know,
> in paths they have not known
>   I will guide them.
> I will turn the darkness before them into light,
>   the rough places into level ground.
> These are the things I do,
>   and I do not forsake them. (Isaiah 42:16)

Someone is out there praying for someone like you to enter their darkness. Don't do outreach. Be it.

TWELVE

MENTORING THAT MATTERS

*A mentor is someone who allows you
to see the hope inside yourself.*

OPRAH WINFREY

"After losing my pops, I met my 'big sis,' Amy," shares Luis. "She moved on our block and embraced us and opened her doors to us. It took us away from our struggle and the reality of street life, if only for an hour or two.

"We were in survival mode. While everybody else didn't see our worth and was hoping we didn't see it—she seen it and hoped that we seen it too. She seen it for real. For me, it took losing my best friend to gun/gang violence and being locked up

to realize my worth and what I want out of life. I have a son and my life ain't my life anymore. It's my son's. I owe him that much."

Luis and I had a unique relationship when he was young. Often he avoided me. Often we spent hours just talking. I saw the impact of gang life on his life. He spent many years in and out of prison as a juvenile. I would attend court dates with his family, got him a lawyer one time, and chased him down the street when he was on the corner dealing. I would always stop by his house to check on him (and sometimes he would hide in the closet to avoid seeing me). But I saw something special in Luis, and I wasn't giving up.

A NEW DEFINITION

One day I was talking on the phone with one of my youth. I overheard him talking to a friend, telling him he was on the phone with his mentor. The other kid asked, "What's a mentor?"

I was not surprised. I wish I'd had a mentor growing up to pour into me, guide me, listen to me, advise me. Many young people have no idea what it means to have a healthy adult figure in their life as they navigate the difficult years of being a young person. But what kind of mentor do these young people need? What does being a healthy mentor look like? In this chapter, I would like to challenge what we have always believed mentorship looks like.

A mentor can be a wise and trusted counselor or an influential supporter. This is the way the world has always defined mentorship. The problem with this is the hierarchy of relationship—the mentor is the superior. A true authentic mentoring relationship establishes trust and respect for the elder of the two but also understands we are in this relationship together, we learn from each other, and we need each other. As Scripture states, "Because we loved you so much, we were delighted to share with you not only the gospel of God but our lives as well" (1 Thessalonians 2:8 NIV).

My definition of a mentor is a positive adult figure walking life with young people as they journey on their way to discovering *who* they are in this world, *why* they matter, and *what* their God-given purpose is.

When a young person chooses you as a mentor, consider it a huge privilege. Mentoring is more about the relationship and less about giving advice or instructions: "The essence of mentoring is the sustained human relationship: a one-on-one relationship that shows a child that he/she is valued as a person and is important to society."[1] Developing a healthy relationship is more important than teaching specific principles or ideas. Mentoring has more to do with who you are than what you do. It has more do to with what you build than what you know. It's the relationship that your young person keeps coming back to, the trust that is built. And with high-risk youth, we know building trust takes time. To mentor one of these youth, you must be willing to commit and have a ton of patience.

There is no quote as true as this statement from Theodore Roosevelt: "People don't care how much you know until they know how much you care." This is especially true when working with those who have built walls of protection due to trauma, abandonment, and mistrust. It is the consistent and dependable relationship that creates the trust that breaks down walls. When this trust is built, they

> MENTORING HAS MORE TO DO WITH WHO YOU ARE THAN WHAT YOU DO.

seek you for advice and comfort. For some, the walls crumble quickly. There is an immediate need for that person to risk their protective covering in order to have a positive role model in their life. For others, the walls are like a prison that takes a lot of chipping away, tenderly, slowly, until that person decides you are trustworthy and reliable. You have to be willing to be in that relationship for the long haul if that's what it takes to get to the core of a healthy mentoring relationship.

DIFFERENT KINDS OF MENTORS

As a healthy mentor, you must be aware that there are all kinds of mentors in the life of a young person. Let's use the movie *Menace to Society* as an example. This 1993 film set in Los Angeles tells the story of Caine, a young man involved in the gang lifestyle trying to escape it for a better life, but he finds it's not easy. His dad is a drug dealer who beats his mom, a heroin addict who dies of an overdose. Caine is introduced to violence and murder at a young age when his dad shoots a man right in front of him. He ends up living with his grandparents in the gang- and drug-infested projects. Throughout the movie, we are introduced to several men who have become "mentors" to him.

Pernell is a family friend who teaches Caine street life: gives him his first drink, teaches him how to hold a gun, and shows him how to be a hustler. Pernell ends up serving prison time. Caine's grandfather is always slinging Scripture at him and coming down on him but asks an important question that gets him thinking: "Do you care whether you live or die?" Caine responds, confused, "I don't know."

Caine's teacher is the only positive male in his life. He challenges the way Caine thinks and views the world. He doesn't judge or tell Caine what to do; he offers another option, tells him the truth, and lets Caine decide for himself.

Our young people come across many types of adults in their childhood and teen years. Each person has an intention when building a relationship with the youth, and it's not always a beneficial one. We have competition, and we must be the ones who lead our young people on a healthy journey.

But if there is anything I have learned about mentoring, it is worth repeating: We are not the lead actors in a kid's life. We are the supporting role. Caine's teacher models for him how to live as a Black man but allows Caine to have ownership and accountability of his own life. There is no compulsion to control Caine but only to create a safe space for him to be vulnerable and explore. May we all learn from a movie most don't dare to watch.

It was the night before I was to teach a workshop on mentoring and I spent the night anxious. I felt God leading me to use a trick out of Tony Campolo's playbook to get the audience's attention. I was nervous but I was all in.

That day I was looking and feeling really cute. I mean, isn't that half the reason we single women go to conferences? We have to look good just in case our future husband "finds a good thing." Anyway, I had on some new black leather boots that were making me look like I came to do business. I. Looked. Good.

As I was teaching, I felt my Eminem moment coming ("This is your moment . . . "). Before I came to my point I asked the crowd, "Y'all, I just bought these new boots so I could look cute, but they are killing my feet. Would you mind if I took them off for a bit?"

Everyone was so supportive and yelled, "Of course" and "Go ahead, girl."

"Thanks, because these hurt like a b—tch."

Gasps came over the crowd. Mothers were covering their kids' ears. People were murmuring to each other. They didn't know what just happened.

"Ow-eee! Thanks y'all cuz that sh—t was hurting. Now, back to my presentation."

The crowd was still murmuring, and some were getting ready to leave.

"As we mentor, we must remember not to focus on a kid's behavior . . . because I noticed that most of you were more concerned about the fact that I said 'b—tch' and 'sh—t' than the fact that I was in pain. No one asked me about my pain. Y'all were more concerned about how I expressed it. We're not in the business of behavior modification but introducing young people to the God of transformation."

The crowd grew silent and then broke out in hand claps. Some stood up clapping. Others held their heads down in shame.

Too often as mentors we focus on behavior modification instead of life transformation. So what, they curse? Do you ever ask the why instead of judging them for it? Maybe they come from a household that expresses themselves only through cursing. Maybe cursing is how they share their anger or pain. And sometimes, they just want to curse. I get that too. I'm around kids who curse all the time, but I understand the why. When it gets too uncomfortable, I might say something like, "I appreciate your passion. Can we try to use other words to express ourselves, though? You're smart enough for that." The point is we have to focus on the root issue of a person's pain and lead them to the God who heals, not show them a God who's covering his ears.

IMPACTFUL MENTORING

I have the privilege to see and examine many mentoring relationships, mainly as a means to learn how to be a better mentor myself. In all my examining, I've noticed a few things that are missing from many mentoring relationships:

Lack of active listening. Most mentors love to talk, preach, and lecture, but they rarely listen. And when they do listen, it is often to form a response, not to really hear what is being said. I often do this listening exercise when I speak to make my point (try it on someone now):

- Say the word *shop* five times.
- What is another name for a police officer? *Cop.* Say that five times.
- And what do you do when you come to a green light? They will probably say "stop," but the answer is "go"! They weren't listening!

Give it another shot:

- Say the word *silk* five times.
- What is the blanket your grandma makes? *Quilt.* Say that five times.
- And what do cows drink? They will probably say "milk" but the answer is "water"! Were they listening this time?

We must become better listeners. "Good listening is not just about learning what a person is saying but making a commitment to digesting the information they are presenting and responding constructively."[2] We have to intentionally focus on what is being said and respond accordingly—and sometimes a response is not even needed. Sometimes a nonverbal response is enough.

Lack of understanding our role. Here's another reminder that we are not the lead actor in our mentee's life but the supporting role. We have the privilege to be in our mentee's life, and we should act accordingly. Impactful mentors let the mentee be the hero of his or her own life.

Lack of "realness" about this Christian walk. I have too often seen mentors present the fluffy side of Christianity without the truth of how hard this walk can be. I have seen mentors talk one "holy" way with youth but behind the scenes there's messiness all around. Yes, we should have boundaries and youth don't need to know all our business, but they should see what's real. This generation of young people is tired of being lied to and entertained by the church. They want real relationships. They seek truth.

> WE ARE NOT THE LEAD ACTOR IN OUR MENTEE'S LIFE BUT THE SUPPORTING ROLE.

I was sharing with one of my youth girls about sex. I told her it had been years since I had sex, and she was like, "You're one of the strongest people I know."

I exclaimed, "No, I'm not! I'm struggling, girl. That's why I need Jesus to help me. Being single ain't no joke!"

I wasn't going to front like it was easy to not have sex. She needed to know most of us struggle in that area, but we also depend on God to help us through. Impactful mentors are real about this walk.

Too much control and arrogance. Impactful mentors know who is in control and are humbled by that. I tend to think we as Christians can be very arrogant and want to control the narrative of the lives of the ones we serve, to take the credit for successes. I've been there. I've run people away from Christ because of my arrogance and need for control. We always try to have the answer, when sometimes our lack of answers can be more helpful in allowing our mentees to come up with their own solutions.

We have incredible examples of impactful mentoring. The Bible shares many mentor relationships: Jesus to his disciples, Naomi to Ruth (Ruth 1:6-18), Moses to Joshua (Exodus 24:13), Paul to Timothy (Acts 16:3), Elijah to Elisha (1 Kings 19:16), and Eli to Samuel (1 Samuel 3:1). Here's what I have found impactful mentors to understand well:

- What we do is more about building trust and developing a strong relationship than it is about answering questions.
- Mentoring is about allowing God to shape and mold our youth. We just join the journey!
- Mentors allow youth to think, explore, and discover in a safe place where they can fail and still feel valued and worthy.
- We are not expected to know all the answers but to help our youth find their own solutions with our guidance.
- We are called to inspire young people and believe in them even when they can't believe in themselves.
- We learn from each other. The teacher becomes the student, and the student becomes the teacher.

Mentoring is not for the faint of heart. It can build our people or hurt them. We must be willing to look at ourselves honestly and be (and stay) humbled by the Spirit of God, who is the ultimate mentor. God has trusted us with these beautiful relationships; we are stewards of our young people, part of the village raising this generation. It's a big deal. Our young people need us to be the best we can be for them—and we need them to help us become that.

RECOGNIZE THE RED FLAGS

Cross-gender mentoring is a definite calling, but there are many challenges that come with that call. This is where we must be honest with ourselves and others and discuss the red flags that may indicate mentoring the opposite sex is not an appropriate place for us or a safe space for them.

I had the privilege to attend a workshop (twice) led by my dear friend, author and youth ministry expert Marv Penner, who shared the following red flags to watch out for when mentoring someone, especially a young person:

- You are having sexual thoughts or relational fantasies about them.
- You are jealous when you see them spending time with a fellow youth worker—especially if they seem to be deepening their relationship.
- You look for excuses to be together as often as possible and you look forward to your meetings because of how you feel when you are with them.
- Someone who cares about you—a spouse, fellow youth worker, or even one of the other kids in your group—expresses concern about your relationship.
- You find yourself flirting with them and enjoying the power it gives you.
- You often feel self-conscious about how they see you and find yourself hoping that you're making a good impression.
- You find yourself probing for information that is titillating or sexually explicit under the guise of "counseling" them.

- You rationalize feelings of guilt that you have about any of the above, telling yourself that it's no big deal and that nothing wrong could possibly happen.

Red flags are red for a reason. *Stop.* We tend to ignore these warnings or try to pray them away, but if you are struggling with any of these, please seek advice and counseling . . . and end that mentor relationship before it causes more harm. You are not a bad person or mentor for struggling. The best mentors are honest with themselves and others and do something about the issue. Too many ministries have fallen because people were not honest and overlooked such flags.

If you notice red flags in the life of a colaborer, address them, first with that person, then with their supervisor or ministry leader. We are responsible for the care and protection of our mentees and youth. If you see something, say something.

If you are a mentor, one of your roles is to act as a resource broker. You are responsible for showing your mentees how to access the services and assistance they need. You should know your community and its resources like the back of your hand. You should know what's happening, what organizations provide specific services, and what churches offer young people.

As someone who mentors youth in prisons, I am aware of what reentry organizations are in the returning communities to help my boys when they come home. It is not for me to re-create the wheel. If there is an organization that does the work of re-entry, instead of connecting my mentee with a ton of resources, I connect them with one organization that can offer all the services. My mentorship includes making sure the organization is doing the work, that my young person is doing what they need to do, and then filling in the gaps. My main job, though, is to know what is out there and available for families and the young people I serve. Connecting them to a lifeline.

■ ■ ■

When I started the Humboldt Park Playerz, we had practice twice a week, and Coach David was serious about the team. Coach David came up with a contract that all players agreed to and signed. He worked them hard and they weren't used to it. One day practice was coming to an end and one of the players, Dee, hadn't been doing what he needed to do the whole practice. He was slacking off, being lazy, and challenging the adults. He violated his contract.

We presented him with the options: to participate and do the activity or leave for the week and not play in that week's game. He got extremely upset and started yelling and cursing at us. David held his cool and said, "It's pretty simple, and it's completely your choice." Dee walked out on the team and didn't return.

That same week I went to the block to check on the boys. As I was standing on the street with some of the guys, I heard in the distance, "Amy Killa! Amy Killa!" In gang language, when a gang wants to challenge their "opps" (opposition), they yell the name of the gang with "Killa" at the end as a threat that they're going to kill, hurt, or harm that gang. It's a phrase that shows who the gang's rivals are and who they're targeting for violence. This young man was threatening me and warning me to watch my back because he was planning to harm me.

The boys who were with me started telling me Dee was saying it all over the block because of what happened at practice. He was trying to scare me, but I wasn't scared. I asked the boys to tell me where he was so I could go talk to him. No one knew.

The next day, same scenario, but no one could find Dee.

The next day, I went to the block and saw Dee. He tried to hide, but I caught him. I confronted him about what he was saying to everyone. He broke down and told me how hurt he was that he was kicked off the team (which we didn't do).

"I was hurt and mad and kinda jealous of the other guys," he admitted. "I didn't want you coming around here anymore, so I threatened you, hoping to scare you away."

"You know, as sad as that is, I understand you," I said. "But we want you on the team. You made a choice. It was your choice."

"Yeah, I get that now," he nodded.

"And another thing," I said. "I'm not going anywhere . . . and don't you ever threaten me again. I know people in very low places." We busted out laughing and ended with a hug.

The next day he called me and asked me if he could go to church with me. To which I responded, "Of course! Devil Killa! Devil Killa!" (he told me never say that again).

Mentoring is about looking *through* the pain, not at it. It's about asking the right questions and getting to the root of a young person's behavior. Had I not looked past Dee's reaction and become angry with him, this moment would have never happened.

Here is my pledge as a mentor, which comes from an unknown author:

I will listen to you with my heart as well as my ears.

I will use the benefit of my experience to guide you.

I will challenge you to find your talents.

I will help you recognize opportunity.

I will find the best in you.

I will not judge you.

I will not lie to you or for you.

I will not do it for you.

I will not accept less than your best efforts.

I will not accept excuses.

I will not give up on you.

I will always pray for you.

I will be someone you can count on.

I will walk life with you.

Here's my addition:

I will always remind you that you are loved and created by God for a purpose!

THIRTEEN

WHAT I'VE LEARNED ABOUT GANG MEMBERS AND GANG CULTURE

I have never seen a hopeful person join a gang.

FATHER GREG BOYLE

As someone who spends a lot of time around gang members, I am often asked how I can hang around them and whether I support their lifestyle. The simple answer is no. I do not justify or accept the gang lifestyle and all that comes with it—the drugs, the drug business, the guns, the violence. What I do support are the young people, whether they are in love with the streets, simply surviving, lost in that world, or

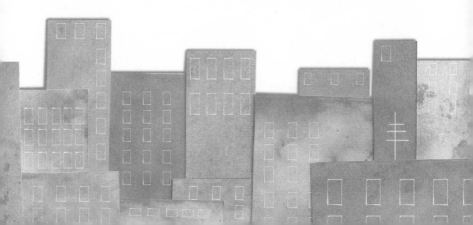

wanting a different life for themselves. I don't agree with it, but I understand.

This chapter is not about revealing all the secrets of gang membership or telling the behind-the-scene business of how gangs operate. That would put me and my young people at risk, and honestly, you can research a lot of that information. I want to share with you what you can't Google. I would like to share with you things I would have never known had I not built relationships with those in gang leadership or gang membership.

GANG MEMBERS ARE HUMAN BEINGS

I know this seems to be a "well, duh" thing to say, but by the way gang members are treated, it seems like people tend to forget this fact. Before they are gang members, they are people first. At the core of who they are, they too are created in the image of God. They were once babies held close by their mothers. They were once toddlers learning how to walk. They were once children with dreams of being firemen, teachers, policemen, and princesses. No one is born with plans to be a gang member.

> THEY ARE HUMANS WHO DESIRE THE SAME THINGS WE DO: TO BE LOVED, TO BE SEEN, AND TO HAVE A HEALTHY LIFE.

At some point as that young person was trying to grow up to be a healthy individual, something happened that threw them off that path. It may have been trauma (which affects brain development), abuse, abandonment, fatherlessness, neglect, poverty, addiction, an absent mother, generational dysfunction, or any of the numerous other reasons so many of our young people decide to join a gang. But in their most vulnerable state, they are humans who desire the same things we do: to be loved, to be seen, and to have a healthy life. As Father Greg Boyle says, "Even gang members imagine a future that doesn't include gangs." And we are called to see them in their humanity *first*, the way God sees them.

MOST GANG MEMBERS AREN'T VIOLENT

The assumption is that every gang member is a homicidal maniac out there shooting and killing people. In fact, many gang members are just hanging on the corner, hanging out at the trap house getting drunk or high or making money. Can they be violent? Absolutely. Every single one of them. Can't you be too, though? It's in all of us to be violent.

Not every member is assigned the role of shooter, but every member needs to be ready to be called upon to do so. We have learned from movies that gang members just sit around all day and plan violence, when in actuality, gang life can be pretty boring, according to several of my young people. Violence does happen, but not every member is planning on committing violent acts.

GANG LEADERS DON'T WANT
THEIR MEMBERS TO DIE

We know that with this lifestyle the loss of life is predictable. I myself have buried over twenty youth due to gang and gun violence, but I know of others whose count is much higher. I know a gang leader who knows hundreds of people who have passed away due to gun violence. He shared with me this fact: "People act like we rejoice in having lost any of our members. *No!* They are our family. We don't want them to die either. That's a heavy burden to bear."

Though we all know death is a risk of membership, not one gang member wants any of their homies to lose their life to the streets.

GANG MEMBERS ARE PROFESSIONAL MOURNERS

Gang members stay in a constant state of grief. They experience loss the same way we do but probably even more intensely than the average person. They lose one person and barely have time to grieve that loss before they start grieving another. Imagine being in a constant state of grief.

One member said his heart just hardened. He felt nothing anymore. "Loss is the norm, and you just keep it moving."

We know grief is a process and has many stages, but imagine being stuck at the anger stage. The depression stage. Never really healing because you are facing loss compounded. One of my dearest mentors, Carol Sato, shared her wisdom with me after the loss of one of my youth: "Grief waits for you. You are going to grieve whether it's today or ten years from now."

I found this statement to be true. The body will force you to grieve at some point—but what if your body doesn't have time? You find creative ways to cope with the grief, and in most cases it usually isn't healthy—drinking, drugs, addiction. Other unhealthy ways could be staying in that constant state of anger, depression, or hardness of heart. There is fear of becoming close to someone again; there is loneliness. Being a professional mourner is how many cope with life.

GANGS AREN'T JUST A CITY PROBLEM

Gangs exist everywhere in this country. If you visit smaller towns, you can see signs of gang activity there as well. Many huge gangs in the city branch out to start factions in these smaller areas.

When I was speaking with a gang leader, he told me of towns where his gang was set up, in states like Idaho, Iowa, and Wisconsin, to name a few. When I speak across the country, I hear of gang issues in rural areas and many suburbs outside of urban areas. These gangs experience the same issues that lead to the formation of gangs in larger cities, such as poverty, boredom, drugs, and systemic racism. They are just as committed and dedicated as the gangs in larger cities.

MEMBERS CAN LEAVE

There is the myth that once a gang member, always a gang member. This is not true. According to studies, the average span of a teenager's gang membership is two years. Though many choose to stay longer, there is always an out. This can be done in many ways, from a head-to-toe "violation" (a two- to four-minute beatdown by members of the gang) to being "blessed out" (if you have become religious) and other ways. Many simply outgrow their gang and start new lives with no consequences from the gang they've left.

I once had a conversation with a gang leader who was going to let a young man out because of the relationship he had with me—but there were rules to him leaving, such as he could never return and he could never come back to the block he served. He had a way out, but unfortunately, he chose to stay and lost his life. I have negotiated with gang leaders for youth who wanted to leave—sometimes successfully, other times not. In one instance, we were not able to get a youth out of the gang without him taking the violation. We had to wait around until they were done and we immediately took him to the hospital. I wrestle with that one every day. How could I have just waited while he was getting a beatdown? Was there nothing I could do? Should I have called the cops? That would have put me and the others at risk. This was part of the consequence of gang membership.

Once someone leaves a gang, there are things they need in order to find success. Top needs include an education program, job or skills training, an actual job, legal help for past issues, tattoo removal, new clothes (many only have clothes with their gang colors or symbols), housing, possible relocation services, and a mentor to walk life with them, teach them, guide them, and hold them accountable. They are pretty much starting life over.

I wish I could bust some more myths, but my safety may be threatened if I do. Instead, I share these few myths as a way for you to see the humanity in this special group. I have learned more from gang members than probably any group I have associated with. I am made all the better and wiser as a result and am so thankful for the role they play in my life, and the role I get to play in theirs.

I understand why young people join gangs. One of the main reasons is that gangs give them a place in society after they are denied a sense of belonging by their parents or community. There are many reasons they join,[1] but the grooming often starts early.

One day I was on the block with the younger shorties, ages four to nine. It was a hot summer day, and I was sitting on my front stoop. I was watching as the young kids ran the street, laughing, playing, throwing water balloons. Then we all heard the famous song ringing through the air—the ice cream truck. You would think they would all run up to the truck, but all the kids ran up to the gang leader. He gave them all money to get what they wanted.

I had seen him in the past buying other things for the younger boys. I walked up to him and said, "So, I get it. This is how the grooming happens. I see. I see." (I know—now that I think about it, that was stupid).

"Not at all," he said. "I'm just buying them ice cream. They don't have any money and I do. You want some ice cream too?"

"Naw, I got my own money."

But the fact that they ran up to him without a blink means he's done that on many occasions. When kids look to the gang member on the block because their needs aren't being met, that is a problem.

Gangs can serve as an alternative family when the immediate family isn't functioning in a healthy manner. There is an intense emotional connection and loyalty to each other when people are part of the same organization. It is a sense of belonging, connection, identity, and, sometimes, financial need. They look to each other for support and brotherhood. They try to be the family they wish they had.

Luis wanted to share his story of why and how he joined the gang, but he wanted to make sure he didn't glorify the lifestyle.

"I won't, Luis," I promised during the phone call to prison. "This is for information purposes only. Why did you join the gang so young?"

"That was all that was around me since I was born," he said. "My dad, the neighborhood, school. It's all I saw; it was the norm."

Luis shared how he and his closest friends used to be a skateboard crew. As they got older, they started riding bikes instead and were more exposed to the streets.

"We would see the old heads and we had no real positive male figures to look to, so we just gravitated towards that," said Luis. "We were poor and we needed money, and they offered to help us make fast money, a lot of it. So, we started hustling and eventually just 'tuned out' and joined the gang, not knowing the bigger picture. So, then, if one of us did it, our boys would follow for fear of missing out."

"Man, I hate I didn't listen to you sooner, Amy," Luis reflected.

Luis and his three brothers all joined a Latino gang organization and spent all of their youth in and out of prison. At times all five of them were locked up. I spent a lot of time going to court, visiting, and spending time with their mom and sister. All in an effort to show these young people there is a better life waiting for them and someone who believed in them.

I've never told a kid to leave the gang. That would be like me telling you to leave your family. To many youth, the gang is the only family they know. Many youth have to sleep on the gang's trap house couch because their family kicked them out. And the gang feeds and clothes them. They feel a deep loyalty and do anything the gang needs them to do.

But sometimes they do choose to leave. Reasons for leaving a gang include aging out, meeting a positive role model, losing someone close, moving or leaving the state, finding employment, pursuing education, raising a family, joining the military, going to prison or death. I've also seen many young men leave the gang because they met a woman who laid down the law: me or the gang. Yes, the power of a woman.

Leaving a gang doesn't happen because someone tells them to. The gang has to leave their heart before they pursue a better life. They have to truly want it before they are ready to step away and walk into the unknown. I always tell my youth, "I know you're not ready, but when you are, I am here and ready to help you start over. Your mind must arrive at the destination before your life does." All I can be is available until that moment happens.

Street gang specialist Rev. Mike Ramey of the Gang Line states it perfectly:

If you put a gang member into a GED/diploma program . . .

> you're breeding an educated gang member.

If you put a gang member into an athletic program . . .

> you'll have an athletic gang member.

If you remove tattoos from a gang member . . .

> you still have a gang member.

If you put a gang member into a jobs program . . .

> you have an employed gang member.

If you put a gang member on probation/parole . . .

> you have short-term compliance, not obedience.

So, what should be the main aim of your programs and relationships? Get youth or gang members to come to themselves— like the prodigal son—and get them willing to see the need to change themselves and their behavior from the inside out. Once their heart changes, then you have an active participant ready to change the trajectory of their life.[2]

■ ■ ■

I once heard an analogy: You're holding a cup of coffee when someone comes along and bumps into you or shakes your arm, making you spill your coffee everywhere.

Why did you spill the coffee?

"Because someone bumped into me!" you reply.

Wrong answer.

You spilled the coffee because there was coffee in your cup. Had there been tea in the cup, you would have spilled tea. Whatever is inside the cup is what will spill out.

Until a person finds healing from their wounds and insecurities, they will be toxic or a burden to every person they run into. Fear can turn into anger, and it spills out in the form of violence. But violence isn't the problem; it's only a root cause of something deeper going on inside that person. We must address the root causes, not put a Band-Aid on the surface issue.

I try to go as deep with a young person as they will allow me to, to express their hurt and pain and show me the root cause. This can be a healing moment for them. If they desire to go further in that journey, I support them but recommend a therapist who can not only go deeper but offer solutions and coping strategies. Until then, I let love spill out.

MENTORING GANG YOUTH

Mentoring youth in gangs is not for the faint-hearted. It's a popular, trendy ministry—until it's not. A lot of people want to be the ones to help a gang member out of the gang until they see all that it takes to make that happen. When I volunteered for a ministry called Urban Life Skills back in 2008 that focused on youth in gangs, there was a process you had to complete before being assigned as a mentor. You had to come to programming four Fridays in a row. As I'm sure you can imagine, we lost a lot of volunteers who found it takes more than four Fridays to connect with these youth.

Here are some things I want to share about mentoring youth in gangs:

- Pursue them and be creative! Don't always wait for them to come to you.

- Go where they are (no fear and no judgment)—but be wise. I was fortunate enough to have a relationship with a gang leader who would call me if something was about to go down to tell me to stay off the block or go home. Have wisdom as to when to show up on the block.

- Have a consistent presence. If you're only around once a month, the impact will be minimal, if any.

- Get it out of your head that they have to physically be in church in order for you to mentor them—no pressure from you! They may never step foot in your church. Does that stop us from making an impact?

- Expose them to options and opportunities. I remember having youth who grew up in Chicago but had never been downtown. I had youth in North Carolina who had never been to the beach (I loved watching them step in the sand and water for the first time). Expose them to new experiences to show them the world is bigger than their block.

- Be willing for it to take as long as it's going to take—and even longer. Gang youth are like a Tootsie Pop or Blow Pop. They have a hard exterior but a tender inside. Trauma can cause them to protect themselves from having anyone gain access to their hearts. I have found the hardest, toughest gang member has the most trauma and is incredibly tender on the inside. The question is, are you willing to take as long as it takes to get the center or will you just bite through it and possibly damage the center?

- I was always careful of the colors I wore and the messages on my T-shirts. I didn't want to associate with any one gang by "reppin' their colors" or their opps' colors. Safety first.

- Be aware of your surroundings and where you take youth. They are not safe everywhere, and you need to know what areas are off-limits. I don't take shortcuts in the city but only drive down well-populated, well-lit, busy main streets. When we had the basketball team, we drove a van with tinted windows and parked right next to the door so the youth could go right inside with no danger. We didn't give the address of the location we were taking them to so they couldn't tell others and take the risk of opps finding out. We were always aware of our environment and took as many precautions as we could to keep our youth safe.

Not all gang members want to be "saved" or rescued—but many do want a lifestyle change. We have a unique opportunity to reach and walk with young people who are lost in gangs and the criminal justice system. Just remember, someone is out there praying for someone like you to enter their darkness. "I have come into the world as light, so that whoever believes in me may not remain in darkness" (John 12:46). Will you answer the prayer?

FOURTEEN

LAND OF THE FREE? INCARCERATION NATION

Don't judge my choices when you didn't see my options.

FORMER CHICAGO GANG MEMBER

"I have never felt so alone, so dehumanized, so unseen, so lost since I've been in prison," Billy said. "This doesn't feel like punishment; it feels like torture. I am human too, you know."

Reminder: I have never been in prison and do not speak on behalf of those who have been. My goal is to share what I have learned from the incarcerated and share my experience with those I've worked with. As we explore this area, may we have eyes to see and ears to listen.

Roddy didn't want visitors his first couple of years in prison. He didn't want people he loved seeing him this way: behind bars, alone, mad, sad. It took some convincing for him to let me come visit. A six-hour drive from the city, my mentee Shalom and I packed up the car and drove down for the weekend. As we were headed down, I was both excited and nervous. Roddy and I talked on the phone. We wrote letters. But it had been years since he was part of the program I worked for, years since I had seen or hugged him. But I pushed the anxiety aside and let it fuel my excitement.

After being patted down and questioned, I was escorted inside to a very hot visiting room with one huge blowing fan. After I'd been waiting anxiously for about thirty minutes, Roddy walked through the door. He was nice and "crispy." Hair was perfect, clothes fresh and "pressed." I immediately started crying happy tears. He approached me and I went in for the hug. The hug was awkward, as if he had forgotten how to do it. Consider he had gone years without physical touch—no hugs, nothing. Maybe he did forget. Maybe it was uncomfortable. Or maybe it was exactly what he needed, and he just didn't know how to receive it. I grabbed him tight through the awkwardness and whispered "It's okay, Roddy. It's me. You're safe."

After six hours together, it was time to say goodbye. I was coming back the next day, so we both had something to look forward to. As we left, I asked, "Can I give you a hug?" He said of course. He hugged me so tight he didn't want to let go. Such a contrast from the first awkward hug. I left and sat in my car and cried. "Lord, may Roddy know he is loved." I think my hugs let him know a little.

As of March 2023, the United States has the highest rate of incarceration of any country in the world. These systems hold almost 2 million people in 1,566 state prisons, 98 federal prisons, 3,116 local jails, 1,323 juvenile correctional facilities, 181 immigration detention facilities, and 80 Indian country jails, as well as in military prisons, civil commitment centers, state psychiatric hospitals, and prisons in the US territories.[1] While the United States represents about 4.25 percent of the world's population, it houses around 22 percent of the world's prisoners. In 2021, about 421,000 people entered prison gates, but people went to jail almost 7 million times. Mass incarceration mostly affects Black and Brown communities. There are more Black men in prison today than there were slaves in 1850. One million children are arrested each year, with 500,000 youth sent to over 1,500 juvenile detention facilities across the country.[2]

And every year, 626,000 people walk out of prison gates—to return back to our communities, many with hopes to try to live better. They need us. We need them. Let's enter the walls.

A five-second look and a smile can change a young person's mood when he's headed to court. When waiting behind the doors to see a judge in court, that individual is anxious to see who came to support him or her during their court date. As soon as they enter the courtroom, the first thing they do is look around to see who is there. That five-second eye contact and smile is sometimes all they have to know they are not alone. Many have parents who can't attend court dates or trials (because of work schedules, taking care of other children, or they simply don't care). Some young people have no one in the audience for them. What a powerful opportunity for a mentor! Even if it's only for five minutes because of a continuance or a five-hour trial, letting a young person know they are not alone reflects the very Spirit of God.

THE PRISON VISITS

Every week I spend many hours visiting youth who are locked up in a jail facility as they anxiously await their trials. I prepare my mind to go through a grueling process in order to spend just fifteen minutes with them.

The process in Chicago goes something like this: Drive to Cook County Jail and try to find parking (which you have to pay for), hoping you put enough money in the meter. You never know how long it will take to go through the process of seeing the inmate, and many of us have gotten parking tickets. Then comes standing in the first line, waiting . . . waiting. . . . waiting. You hear babies crying, family members complaining, young people cursing and saying what they would do if they were locked up, teen girls bragging about what their boyfriend did to get locked up. Many are quiet and brokenhearted. I find myself helping others who have never been through the process and trying to make them feel as comfortable as possible.

Then comes the first security check. I have learned to bring only my key (no key chain) with my ID, but they still search you—even run their hands quickly between your breasts to see if you're hiding something there (I always feel so *violated)*. And I get mad seeing them frisk babies and children. You go to the division and wait in another line to give your inmate's name, show your ID, and explain your relationship to the inmate.

Then you sit and wait. This could be anywhere from thirty minutes to two hours, and you wait with other visitors who are agitated by being treated by jail staff like they are the prisoner. No books, no magazines, no music, no cell phone. You just sit and wait. Then they call your name and the inmate's name and you go through a *second* search: another pat down, another chance to feel violated.

Then you walk into the visitors' rooms, choose a thick glass window (a nasty, dirty, germ-infested window that hasn't been cleaned probably ever), and wait for your "inmate"—knowing you can't comfort them with an embrace, only with a smile.

M. Santos shares on his blog how he prepared for visitors while in prison:

> My ritual to prepare for the Saturday morning visit began the night before, when I would lay my pants and shirt carefully beneath my sleeping mat on the concrete platform that served as my bed. The weight of my body through the night would press creases into the drab clothing, and I hoped the effort would make me look sharp. I'd wake early. By knocking out several hundred pushups on the floor of my cell, I could get my blood pumping, swell my muscles, hopefully giving the illusion of strength. I'd take a bird-type bath in my sink, shave closely, then pull on my jail outfit, methodically folding up my sleeves to flaunt what I thought were impressive biceps. Then I sat on the corner of my bed, minimizing movement so as not to wrinkle my clothes, and waited for jailers to escort me to the visiting booth.[3]

Once you are facing your inmate, you get fifteen minutes for your visit.

Fifteen minutes to love them.

Fifteen minutes to encourage them.

Fifteen minutes to laugh with them.

Fifteen minutes to listen to them.

Fifteen minutes to give them hope.

Fifteen minutes to let them know they are not alone.

This time together is exhausting, emotional, and important to the ones you are visiting who desire a tender look and genuine smile. As Santos's blog states, "Visits in the jail couldn't alleviate the anxieties I felt, but they helped. Instead of focusing on the seemingly interminable judicial proceedings, I could look forward to the friendly faces and voices; those visits gave me support when I needed it most."[4]

A friend of mine shared with me that these visits are exhausting. Afterward the emotional and physical wear on the body can take hours or days to recover from. Many people experience deep depression and extreme exhaustion, sleeping a lot after a visit in an attempt to recover from the emotions they have experienced. Santos continues, "A crushing hangover always followed my time in the visiting booth, but within a few days, I'd welcome the familiar anticipation building while I waited to see my family again."[5]

It's a Catch-22, but I can't imagine not spending time with my youth as they sit alone day after day, waiting for a decision that can change their life.

There is a reason Scripture clearly states, "Remember those who are in prison, as though in prison with them, and those who are mistreated, since you also are in the body" (Hebrews 13:3). Many are forgotten once they get behind bars. I've heard it said that when someone first gets locked up, they get tons of visits and letters. After about three months, that's cut in half. After three more months, that gets cut in half. Eventually, it's just two or three people writing and visiting—their mom and a girlfriend or boyfriend and maybe a mentor. They feel forgotten but we know that's not true. God cares for them as he cares for us. God sees them—their trauma, their loneliness, their regret, their pain. He also sees their lives as valuable. I am always amazed at how God has their attention when they are isolated from their normal lives. It is a beautiful time to let them know of God's love and hope for their lives.

Yes, many are in prison for a reason. Many are also innocent. All of them are seen by God as his children. Visits and letters are a lifeline to the incarcerated. It reminds them of their humanity and value.

One weekend I visited a young man in prison. Our visit was wonderful. We talked about everything you can imagine. We got to hug. I was able to buy him food. We laughed. We cried. We connected. He thanked me for

> **REMEMBER THOSE WHO ARE IN PRISON, AS THOUGH IN PRISON WITH THEM, AND THOSE WHO ARE MISTREATED, SINCE YOU ALSO ARE IN THE BODY.**
> *Hebrews 13:3*

taking a full day to come visit with him (a two-hour drive there, an hour in the waiting room, a four-hour visit, and the two-hour drive back home). A week later I got a letter from him: "When it was all said and done, I felt very appreciated, loved, and human—something that I forgot I was—a sense that I hadn't felt in a very long time. It was difficult to see you go."

∎ ∎ ∎

Eleven hours with Roddy. Over two days I got to spend eleven wonderful hours with him. We didn't think we would have that much to talk about, but we ended up talking nonstop. It was still hot in the visiting room, so this time I chose a table in front of the fan. It was a Sunday and my last day to see Roddy. He walked through the door, and the hug was not awkward this time! But he immediately saw the Bible open on the table and looked at me suspiciously.

"Now you know I don't be doing that, Amy," Roddy said.

"I know you don't, but I do," I shot back. "I am missing church today to be here with you, so we're going to read one Scripture and be done in five minutes."

"I can at least do that for you," he conceded.

We proceeded to read my favorite Scripture, Psalm 139:

For you formed my inward parts;

you knitted me together in my mother's womb.

I praise you, for I am fearfully and wonderfully made.

Wonderful are your works;

my soul knows it very well.

My frame was not hidden from you,

when I was being made in secret,

intricately woven in the depths of the earth.

Your eyes saw my unformed substance;

in your book were written, every one of them,

the days that were formed for me,

when as yet there was none of them.

How precious to me are your thoughts, O God!

How vast is the sum of them!

If I would count them, they are more than the sand.

I awake, and I am still with you. (Psalm 139:13-18)

"Amy?" Roddy said reluctantly.

"Yeah," I answered.

"What do you think God thinks of me?"

On the inside, I was crying and screaming. *Yes! Finally!* On the outside, I was cool as a cucumber. "What a great question," I said.

Roddy and I proceeded to have a deep conversation about God. That five minutes turned into thirty minutes of an unexpected encounter with God for Roddy. My heart still explodes when I think of it.

■ ■ ■

It was time to leave Roddy and head back to Chicago. We didn't want it to end, but it had to after two days together.

"Time's up," yelled the guard, and it seemed to echo all over the facility.

I was fighting tears. I felt nauseous. I was trying to be strong for Roddy. He might not have another visit for months, years even. *Let there be joy, Amy, not sadness.* We hugged tightly. Longer than usual. We both knew we might not see each other for a while.

"Call me tonight when you get the phone," I said. "Be sure you do this. I will be waiting."

He nodded his head yes and he lowered his chin to the ground. He wasn't an emotional young man, and he was fighting it viciously.

"Let's go!" the guard repeated.

Roddy gave me one last hug and was escorted out of the room back to his cell.

"Call me!" I yelled. "Don't forget!"

I know how hard it is for those who are incarcerated to say goodbye to loved ones. I make sure I get them to call me the day of the visit and the day after to help them as much as I can through that experience.

I sat in my car, crying again. This time the sadness was hurting my heart. I was exhausted. I am thankful to Shalom for taking over the driving and listening to me share my heart. Roddy and I grew much closer—and he did call me that evening.

One of my youth, Marc, and I had a life-changing conversation over Securus, the prison communication system where you pay for phone calls, emails, and video visits. He was coming home within a month, and he was extremely anxious. As we talked, I suggested that he was anxious because he didn't have a plan. After thinking about it, he agreed. I gave him some homework and we began working on a plan. The relief he felt was clear even over the phone.

The two questions he had to answer were:

1. List three people in your life who can help you stay on track and hold you accountable.

2. List three people in your life who, if you hang out with them, will take you off your focus.

"Amy, I have to be honest," Marc started. "That second question, I have a long list. That first question, I only have one positive person in my life—and that's you. Not even my mom or dad. They are on the same BS I was on when I was in the street. I need more positive people."

"Well, no wonder you ended up in where you are," I exclaimed. "There is a whole new world just waiting to be opened up to you, and there are some pretty amazing people I know who can walk with you too. I can't wait for you to meet them—and bring some of your friends along, too."

We can never assume young people have a team of support around them. We must become that team for them.

TOO MANY CHOICES

Roddy was home and having a hard time adjusting. The first thing his dad did was give him a beer before he got a single hug. He had gone to prison as a boy and come out as a man who had no idea how to do life on the outside.

One day he asked me to take him to get his ID. As we were heading over to the DMV, I noticed Roddy was acting a little different. He was very anxious, shaking his leg, tapping his knees, his breathing elevated.

I reached over to touch his shoulder. "Are you okay?" I asked. "There's no rush. We can do this another day."

"Naw, let's get it over with," he said.

"Okay," I said. "I'm here."

We walked into a busy DMV. The lines were long, the staff were shouting, and only a few seats were available. It was chaotic. Roddy was overwhelmed. His anxiety was at an all-time high. He wanted to be in and out—but as we all know, the DMV moves at a snail's pace. I walked closely with him at every step and made sure he was safe. At one point he needed to go outside for fresh air to calm down. He got his ID. As we sat in the car, I asked him what he was feeling.

"Relieved it's over," he said as he took a deep breath.

When people come home after being incarcerated, we seem to think that as long as they have a job, a place to live, and food on the table, they'll be fine. But rarely does anyone talk about the trauma of institutionalization and social reintegration.

Institutionalization creates difficult and problematic transitions as people return to the free world. For example, one of my youth said going to the grocery store was a horrible experience. There were too many choices. He wasn't used to having a choice. He got what he got when they wanted him to have it. A grocery store was not a space where he felt safe or in control.

Another friend shared his experience at Subway, where every step of getting a sandwich is a choice. Choice of bread. Choice of meat. Choice of toppings. Choice of sauce. It was too overwhelming and he screamed at the teenage worker, "Just give me my effin sandwich!"

Choice is not a luxury on the inside; it's barely a right. One youth shared that when given a choice in prison, many people are afraid they will make the wrong choice and therefore give up their option to choose anyway.

In a report titled "From Prison to Home: The Effect of Incarceration and Reentry on Children, Families, and Communities," author Craig Haney discusses the psychological changes many prisoners are forced to undergo in order to survive the prison experience. Haney defines the term *institutionalization* as "the process by which inmates are shaped and transformed by the institutional environments in which they live. . . . In general terms, the process of prisonization involves the incorporation of the norms of prison life into one's habits of thinking, feeling, and acting."[6] We can agree that confinement in horrible conditions can cause long-term psychological effects on anyone.

"When most people first enter prison, of course, they find that being forced to adapt to an often harsh and rigid institutional routine, deprived of privacy and liberty, and subjected to a diminished, stigmatized status and extremely sparse material conditions is stressful, unpleasant, and difficult," Haney continues.

But this new state soon becomes "increasingly 'natural,' second nature, and, to a degree, internalized." It becomes a new way of thinking, behaving, and acting. Many people in prison aren't even aware they are becoming institutionalized, and our communities are not prepared to "absorb the high level of psychological trauma and disorder that many will bring with them" when they return to our communities.[7]

"The excessive *and* disproportionate use of imprisonment over the last several decades also means that these problems will not only be large but concentrated primarily in certain communities whose residents were selectively targeted for criminal justice system intervention," Haney states.[8] The need for resources is critical if we want healthy individuals, families, and communities. We need to create transitional and transformational programs ("effective decompression programs"[9]), and those who are currently and formerly incarcerated need a seat at the table when these programs are created and implemented.

Most incarcerated youth and adults are coming home, back to their communities. May we create communities that welcome them, see them, and help further their healing journey as they take the next steps to a healthy life. We can become a supportive community, create a reentry ministry, start small groups for returning citizens, direct them to resources for the physical needs they will have, offer rides to prisons for families, offer returning-home care packages with toiletries, and the list goes on. The world looks to the church for healing and love. These are a few ways we can provide those for returning citizens.

INVISIBLE PUNISHMENTS

Even though men and women across the country serve sentences for the crimes they were charged with, when they come home, it's as if they enter another prison. Invisible punishments are those systems in place to remind the formerly incarcerated and society that this person was an inmate, has a past, and doesn't deserve a second chance. Social exclusion. Collateral consequences. This plays out in forms such as housing limitations, limited (if any) voting rights, lack of access to employment, education, or business licensing, and so on. We constantly remind those who have served their time that they are still criminals in society's eyes—second-class citizens.

As the church we must lead the charge in changing this narrative. If the church is about forgiveness, grace, and new life, we should be the ones who welcome our returning citizens home with resources and a place to belong. We must advocate on behalf of those who have grown during their time on the inside and want to live a healthier life. We must represent the God of second, third, and hundredth chances. We must advocate for laws to be changed that allow these harmful practices to limit the lives of reformed returning citizens.

> IF THE CHURCH IS ABOUT FORGIVENESS, GRACE, AND NEW LIFE, WE SHOULD BE THE ONES WHO WELCOME OUR RETURNING CITIZENS HOME.

Gio came home at the age of twenty-one after serving six years in a juvenile prison to live with his mother. One day he called me frustrated, angry, and hopeless.

"I was a boy in that prison," he exclaims. "Now I'm a man? I'm a boy in a man's body. I don't know how to do this life. The system didn't teach me how to grow up . . . and when I ask for help, no one wants to help me. Society wants me to be a man, but they won't give me a chance. Everywhere I go, they remind me I was locked up. How am I supposed to do better if I can't even get a chance?"

Language is power. What you call someone sticks with them. The old childhood rhyme "Sticks and stones may break my bones, but words will never hurt me" is a lie we like to tell ourselves. I am very careful in what I call or name people. I don't use the words *felon*, *ex-con*, or *ex-offender*. I prefer to say, "He is a person with a felony record," or, "She is a person with a criminal background." I lead with person-centered language because that's what we should see first. I would never want someone to see me only as the mistakes or bad choices I have made. I am a person first—just as God sees me. I find this kind of language can reduce the stigmatization of returning citizens and humanize their existence. Isn't that the heart of God?

"I'm coming home soon and my whole life flashed in front of my eyes. It made me count my blessings and I understood that from the moment I was born, my life has had meaning. I'm not alone."

From Luis to young people reading this:

Always have faith. You're never alone, even in your darkest moments. There is someone there for you dying to help you. Our past, our struggle, where we come from, should never define our future. It's OK to make mistakes but learn from them, learn from the mistakes of others like me. This ain't the life you want. If you have an Amy in your life, don't run from her. Run *to* her. It's time to break the cycle. Embrace your talent and secure your future. I love you, Big Sis. You forever changed my life.

And from the author of Hebrews to us:

> Remember those who are in prison, as though in prison with them, and those who are mistreated, since you also are in the body. (Hebrews 13:3)

PART TRES

SEEING YOURSELF

FIFTEEN

THE GREAT I AM . . . NOT

God said to Moses, "I AM WHO I AM."

EXODUS 3:14

Hi. My name is Amy, and I am a recovering fourth member of the Trinity.

Welcome, Amy!

My story is pretty basic. For many, many years I was under the assumption that when it came to my life and the life of others, it was my input, my views, my opinions, and my well-thought-out strategic plans (typed, double-spaced, and in twelve-point Times New Roman font) that was needed for the universe to revolve and the lives of people around me to be changed (through Jesus Christ, my Lord and Savior, of course). I just knew God

had chosen me because of my hardcore life experiences, my unlimited victories, my invaluable wisdom, my impressive résumé, and my undeniable success rate when it came to giving others advice.

I just knew God was impressed with me and my works. Therefore, it merited an executive position as the fourth member of the Trinity alongside the Father, the Son, and the Holy Spirit. (I was working on coming up with another name for the group, like "Amy and the Trinity" or "the Trinity plus Amazing Amy.") I admit, I was a little intimidated by all of the responsibility that came with this honor, but because of how fabulous I knew I was (and God knew I was), I was confident I could handle it.

After all, why would God put me in a position of ministering to . . .

- the unlovable and undesirable?
- the hardest hardcore youth in the world?
- gang members who spend more time smoked out on the block than a chimney in a snowstorm?
- adult volunteers who had more drama than the youth I spent time with?
- community leaders whose egos were bigger than a tsunami?
- youth who spend more time in jail than all the combined years they have spent in school?

I'm just saying, of course God thinks I'm incredible! That's why he chose me and not some self-righteous, holier-than-thou Christian who's under the assumption they have the power and ability to change people's lives and save them from themselves! (Insert rolling eyes here.)

Amy . . .

Sorry, am I still speaking in present tense? I am still recovering. Have mercy, Lord. Are we done? I have an SBC (Spoiled Brat Club) meeting to attend next.

WHO I AM NOT

If God is the great I Am, then we are the great I Am Nots—and for that I am thankful. Nothing takes the pressure off me more than knowing who I am and who I am not. And as God calls us to the sacredness of ministry, this is a key principle to understand. Our role in the kingdom comes with many responsibilities, but we must be very clear on what those are. If our role is not clearly defined, we will tend to get in God's way and possibly create more unintentional damage to the people we are called to serve. And none of us want that.

Before we accept our calling, we first need to humble ourselves to recognize how God sees us before we can recognize how God sees others. It starts with how we see ourselves. The truth is, I am a hot mess and I need Jesus. In no way am I close to having the wisdom, knowledge, love, or character of God, but God still chooses to use me for his greater purpose. I am humbled, and always acknowledge, that there

> IF GOD IS THE GREAT I AM, THEN WE ARE THE GREAT I AM NOTS.

is work to be done on myself as I seek to be more like Jesus. The gift is that in that journey, he can still use us—and he does, if we let him. It's still a choice, sometimes an everyday choice.

After my husband left me, it seemed like "our" ministry left with him. He was the one the world saw as the "minister" and I was the wifey, the helper, the assistant. I figured he was the one who was called, so I also figured my time in ministry was up once we split. I never had plans to do ministry again. I decided to be a church member only and focus on a career outside of ministry.

But because I am not the I Am, because I wanted everything God had in store for my life, and because I told God numerous times my life was his, he made a different decision . . . and here I am today, thirty years later (and counting), serving God and loving young people. I now can't imagine my life any other way. He knew and saw that I had a purpose greater than what I had planned. Surrendering to the great I Am requires letting our will be his—even if we can't see the bigger picture.

THE I AM

So, who is this great I Am? The term *I Am* appears over three hundred times throughout the Bible, starting in Exodus and ending in Revelation. God first introduces himself as the I Am to Moses, who had the unthinkable privilege of meeting God at the burning bush. As Moses comes to Horeb, the mountain of God, he sees the burning bush that is not consumed by fire and is curious to understand it. God calls to him from the midst of the bush. God shares that he has heard the cry of his people for deliverance, and he promises he will save them from the hands of the Egyptians. But Moses has doubts—not about God, but about himself. In Genesis 3, God reassures him that *he sees Moses* and has called him to this mission.

> Then Moses said to God, "If I come to the people of Israel and say to them, 'The God of your fathers has sent me to you,' and they ask me, 'What is his name?' what shall I say to them?" God said to Moses, "I AM WHO I AM." And he said, "Say this to the people of Israel: 'I AM has sent me to you.'"

God also said to Moses, "Say this to the people of Israel: 'The LORD, the God of your fathers, the God of Abraham, the God of Isaac, and the God of Jacob, has sent me to you.' This is my name forever, and thus I am to be remembered throughout all generations." (Exodus 3:13-15)

Also note the use of the name "I Am" by Jesus in John 8:58: "Jesus said to them, 'Truly, truly, I say to you, before Abraham was, I am.'"

Shakespeare asks in *Romeo and Juliet*, "What's in a name?" A lot! Names are incredibly significant. Your parents probably took months to figure out what to name you before you were even born—and God's calling himself "I Am" was also well-thought-out.

What is the significance of being called "I Am"? In Hebrew, the passage uses the verb *ehyeh* (from the root *hayah*), normally translated as "I am" or "I will be," but for the meaning in Exodus, we must look further into the word *hayah*. Dr. Michael LeFebvre states, "In biblical Hebrew, the being verb *hayah* conveys not just existence but manifest existence. It indicates the appearance, presence, or standing of a thing."[1] He further explains that God isn't just existing but is "being" and is a "present being" with his people. He is more than just a God in title; he is a God of being.

For me, when I hear God calling himself the "I Am," it means the all-encompassing God meets me exactly where I am, sees me in my need, and shows up as the question, answer, and solution in that very moment or season.

HE IS MORE THAN JUST A GOD IN TITLE; HE IS A GOD OF BEING.

He is with me. I Am has no limitations. I Am is everything to all people. I Am is always with his people.

KNOW YOUR ROLE

How do we let God be God? We often get in his way and foil the plans he has in mind for ourselves and others. The simple answer is: Know. Your. Role. You are not the fourth member of the Trinity (meetings daily all day long for those recovering— see you there). By knowing your role in the kingdom, you allow God to be God. Learn what your role is, what your responsibilities are—and what they are *not*. Take your rightful place but know what that is.

I am the kind of person who likes to be in control—and control is all about fear, needing security and stability. I have found that letting go of control can be scary and liberating at the same time. The liberating part allows me not only to let God be God but to *see* God do what he does best. I love letting God show off, but for that to happen I need to be humble, stay out of the way, and look for ways to be used that don't cloud his glory. I mean, how will others see God if we're always in the way? How will *we* see him?

One of the greatest lessons I have learned while doing ministry is knowing my role, not only in the kingdom but in another person's life. The journey is theirs. It belongs to them, not you. You are blessed to be a small or significant part of that journey. We must allow people the space and time to take that journey by God's timeline, not ours. God has a plan. Trust that! Let God be God in someone's life, whether they have a relationship with him or not. Play your role. Play it well. But know what that role is.

That first late-night call. It's 2:20 a.m.

"Miss Amy, I'm in jail," exclaimed Micah. "Can you please bail me out?"

"I wish I could but I don't have the money," I answered.

I got off the phone trying to think of a way to get him out. I prayed hard . . . and felt God say to me, "Just because you can, doesn't mean you should. Leave this to me."

I am a natural fixer. I like to fix things for people. I like the joy it gives me to know I did something that made a difference. This ego often gets in the way of God's plans. I never want to get in God's way, but I think I do—often—because of my need to be helpful and needed.

Sometimes it's hard to distinguish between what God needs us to do and when we need to take a seat and let God work it out. Should I bond him out? Can I? Yes, I can, but does God want me to? What if God wants that young man to spend one night in jail to see what it's like? What if there is a Christian corrections officer there who knew him growing up and they end up having a life-changing conversation? What if I don't pray or seek direction from God on what to do so I get in the way of a transformational experience? We must seek God fervently in prayer for situations such as these. In most cases, we are still a part of the process, but sometimes we are more involved than we should be. We must learn to let God be God.

Over my years of service, God has taught me a lot about my role, who I am supposed to be in "partnership" with him—and who I am not:

- I am to be a light in someone's darkness.
- I am to be a reflection of God's love.
- I am the supporting (*not* the lead) role in all my relationships.

LIGHT IN SOMEONE'S DARKNESS

> In the same way, let your light shine before others, so that they may see your good works and give glory to your Father who is in heaven. (Matthew 5:16)

Often when we walk with those on the margins, we encounter dark places. We enter dark places. We find ourselves sitting with those who can't find a way out. Because of our hope for them and our relationship with God, we can become a light that shines hope and love. We can help people see a way out by connecting them with the God who sees them and has a plan "to prosper you and not to harm you, plans to give you hope and a future" (Jeremiah 29:11 NIV).

I think of all the conversations I have with my young people who spend hours in an old, dirty, nasty prison cell. I see the toll it takes on them. I can hear it when they call me, when I see them face to face. What a great opportunity to be hope and light to them in such a dark place. John 1:5 states, "The light shines in the darkness, and the darkness has not overcome it." We win! God is the outlet, the source, and we are to be the extension of light in someone's darkness.

A REFLECTION OF GOD'S LOVE

> Beloved, let us love one another, for love is from God, and whoever loves has been born of God and knows God. Anyone who does not love does not know God, because God is love. (1 John 4:7-8)

I am here to show love to all people, especially those who don't know love. As Christian communities we must show love to each other as a model that we know love because we know God, who is love. Unless we love each other, those who don't know God will not be convinced of his love for them. Our love of God is reflected in how we treat people. Period. How can we be a reflection of God's love if we treat others poorly? If we choose not to see others? God's love is a healing balm, and one of my roles is to spread that balm like creamy peanut butter on a piece of smooth white bread.

THE SUPPORTING ROLE (*NOT* THE LEAD)

Do not be arrogant toward the branches. If you are, remember it is not you who support the root, but the root that supports you. (Romans 11:18)

Everyone among you not to think of himself more highly than he ought to think, but to think with sober judgment, each according to the measure of faith that God has assigned. (Romans 12:3)

As mentioned earlier, it is vital that we know our role in the lives of those we serve. We have to love people enough to let God be God in their lives. We don't control the process or the outcome. We are just privileged to be a part of their story.

It is very humbling to be an I Am Not in this world. It puts us in the position of recognizing our limits, our abilities, our talents—and the lack thereof. But mostly it allows us to see God being God. The great I Am can outperform all of us and make things happen. He is the God of healing and transformation beyond anything we could ever do. Being an I Am Not releases us from being God or playing God in another's life.

Take a deep breath in, right now. Release that breath . . . and release the burden you have taken upon yourself to be God. Embrace being the great I Am Not and rest in his love.

SIXTEEN

EMBRACING YOUR CALLING

Know what sparks the light in you so you can illuminate the world.

OPRAH WINFREY

One hot summer day in Chicago, I sat staring out the window of my small three-bedroom apartment on the top floor of a two-flat, looking across the street at three affordable "scattered site housing" units. These units were created throughout Chicago in the 1960s due to a lawsuit from tenants alleging that the Chicago Housing Authority (CHA) was "perpetuating racial segregation by only siting projects in the ghetto." At the time, CHA was building high-rise projects in Black districts only. The new scattered sites were to be built in white communities for the elderly. Soon after, the buildings' poor design and lack of

maintenance led to such extreme deterioration that the US Department of Housing and Urban Development took control of the CHA. Today, most high-rise buildings have been torn down and there are more affordable housing sites throughout the city.

I grew up as a child in Maine. In the country.

I was raised as a teen in North Carolina. In the burbs.

Now as an adult, I live in the concrete jungle of Chicago. In a gang neighborhood.

The vast differences between the three are never-ending, and they have all shaped me profoundly for this ministry journey.

Across from me these worn-down units with tiny front yards had more patches of brown grass than green, and trash was spread over their yards and onto the street. On this day everyone was out in the front yard sitting in whatever little areas of shade they could find trying to cool down. The music was loud. Two kids were chasing each other with water balloons, one screaming as she begged not to be soaked. One mother was shouting to her child to bring her a cold pop (we from New England call it soda) before she came outside. Two teenagers I have started getting to know bought ice cream from the neighborhood ice cream truck whose annoying, blaring music was clashing with the deep bass hip-hop being played in a young man's shiny, just-washed car.

I was observing it all from my air-conditioned living room window. I was annoyed at how loud everything was but loved watching the kids enjoy the summer day. The two teenagers were laughing as they peeled off the wrapping on the ice cream before it melted. Then they threw the wrapper on the ground in their yard.

I was irritated. Why didn't they throw it in the trash bag hanging from the fence? Why would they not care about trashing their home? How could they be so comfortable with disposing of their trash on the ground without a second thought?

"God, I don't understand this hood mentality. *Please* help me to get inside their heads and understand," I begged as I watched with both frustration and a deep desire to "get it."

"God, I can't do this. Why do you have me in this neighborhood? A place I never grew up around. A place I will never truly understand. I can't help anyone if I don't understand this mentality," I said as I continued my conversation with God. "You picked the wrong girl to live in the hood."

And God was silent as I watched the mom with the soda can (or pop for you Midwesterners) toss it into the street.

The next day I was sitting on my concrete stoop in front of the house trying to enjoy the peace and quiet of a Sunday morning. The two teenagers from the day before and their three younger siblings excitedly ran across the street to join me. It was a nice interruption. They had big smiles but were wearing dirty clothes from the day before.

"Miss Amy!" they said with excitement. "It sure is hot out today. You got any brownies?"

"You know I always have brownies," I said enthusiastically. "Come on up and let's get you something cool to drink too."

They weren't used to being invited into someone's home and jumped at the chance. They beat me to the front door! As soon as we entered my air-conditioned apartment, the nine-year-old girl screamed, "This is a mansion!" She ran up and down the hallway looking in each room, yelling for everyone to come look.

I didn't know how to respond. To me, my apartment was not at all what I was used to. It was nice but small, nowhere near the big houses and mansions I had lived in or personally seen in my lifetime.

She fell back with delight on my eggplant-colored couch and said, "This must be nice."

"I do like it," I said. "And when you get older, you can have the same thing. You just gotta keep going to school and work hard."

"Really?" she asked with sincere wonder. "I can live like this, Miss Amy?"

"And you better have me over for dinner when you do!" I exclaimed.

We enjoyed the brownies, cold lemonade, and air conditioning as we all talked about things that didn't really matter. As I escorted them out the door with lots of hugs, I stood on the concrete stoop waving goodbye.

"This is why I chose you," said the Lord. "They don't understand you either, but they need to see something different. You are going to show them a different way."

Many times I have questioned why God would choose someone like me to do this incredibly important work of loving young people in a neighborhood so foreign to me. I had always made it my mission to help young people expand their worldview, but now, here I was having my worldview expanded as well.

I used to believe expanding a young person's worldview meant taking them places they had never been or introducing them to people they would normally never meet. I've taken young people who have lived in Chicago their whole lives but have never been downtown to experience Lake Michigan or the Sears Tower. I've taken young people who lived two hours from the beach to experience the salt air smell or the sand between their toes for the first time. I've introduced young people to CEOs and famous athletes or musicians who have told them they can do anything they put their minds to.

However, I have learned that expanding someone's worldview is also about challenging mentalities in everyday life. In that respect, here I was being taught about another worldview, that of a young person who lived in poverty, teaching me the ways and mentalities of her life. I needed to be taught about her worldview, and this made me a better neighbor and mentor.

I appreciated that day because it not only expanded my worldview but humbled me and showed me more of where I am deficient. When my weaknesses are blaring at me in the mirror, I tend to immediately question God's choice in using me. I begin to remind God of every flaw I possess, like he doesn't know already. Sometimes I pout and become a spoiled little brat. God patiently waits and reminds me that he knows what he's doing and made no mistake in calling me to this work. I wipe the tears and breathe.

We often believe it's our strengths that make us great leaders, but it is our weaknesses that push us to grow, to heal, to move out of the way, and to let God be God. It then becomes more about God getting the glory and credit than our abilities to make things happen. Instead of beating ourselves down or feeling sufficiently incompetent, we should embrace our weaknesses as an opportunity to learn and become what God intends for us to be, to become better neighbors, leaders, and children of God. Will we ever be good enough? The real question is, Does it matter?

> WE SHOULD EMBRACE OUR WEAKNESSES AS AN OPPORTUNITY TO LEARN AND BECOME WHAT GOD INTENDS FOR US TO BE.

YOUR STRATEGIC CALLING

We were all created to glorify God. We are designed "to act justly and to love mercy and to walk humbly with [our] God" (Micah 6:8 NIV). We are created to "go into all the world and proclaim the gospel to the whole creation" (Mark 16:15). And we are created to "use [our gifts] to serve one another, as good stewards of God's varied grace" (1 Peter 4:10-11). "It's in Christ that we find out who we are and what we are living for. Long before we first heard of Christ and got our hopes up, he had his eye on us, had designs on us for glorious living, part of the overall purpose he is working out in everything and everyone" (Ephesians 1:11-12 MSG).

God has a special plan for how you fulfill your calling. He has been strategic in creating you with all your gifts, talents, and personality to fulfill the great mission of loving people and sharing the hope of Jesus. Your calling is very specific to *you*. A calling utilizes your natural gifts and only you can carry it out. It may be working full-time in that field, volunteering on weekends, or starting a business or nonprofit. It can happen in many ways. All you have to do is say, "Yes, Lord," and it begins.

HOW DO I FIND MY CALLING?

I would like to share with you how I discovered my calling: I embraced what I was most passionate about and then made the choice to live my life passionately. What did that mean for me? That meant looking for jobs or volunteer opportunities that fed my passion. Passion comes from God's special design of the person he created. I didn't want to live my life doing something that wasn't stirring my passion. My personal passion is seeing the young people society ignores overcome and thrive. I have been offered and pursued for many executive director positions, but I knew in the end (though the money was good) that it was not the thing that made me want to get out of bed in the morning. My passion was never about being behind a desk but about being on the front lines, on the ground walking with young people one-on-one. Being with young people, being in the prisons and on street corners gave me joy, excitement, meaning—so I pursued that.

Passion keeps you connected. Mentoring gang members is trendy until it isn't . . . until you can't connect with them, or they give you hell and then you reconsider. That's not passion; that's exploration. Passion keeps you in it for the long haul because you know God gave you the calling to make a difference in that area. "The place God calls you to is the place where your deep gladness and the world's deep hunger meet."[1]

Howard Thurman's famous quote goes, "Don't ask what the world needs. Ask what makes you come alive and go do that, because what the world needs is more people who have come alive."[2] So pay attention to where God naturally draws you. What makes your heart flutter and race? What injustice makes you so righteously angry that you want to do something to change it? What can't you stop thinking about? What areas do you have constant ideas about? What makes you want to get out of bed in the morning? You may be connecting with the very thing that is the purpose for your life.

Once you discover what you are most passionate about, find an organization that specializes in that field and see how you can volunteer. Take classes. Ask your church to start a program centered around that. Doors will open. Just get involved in some form or fashion. Feed the passion.

So, what do you do while you're trying to figure out what your calling is? Until God shows you your *what*, just keep loving God, loving people, sharing Jesus. Pay attention and pray. It will come. I promise you.

I knew what God called me to, but everyone else was disagreeing: *You can't work with boys in gangs because you're a woman.* How do you embrace your calling when the world contradicts it? Sometimes it makes you think you are doing the wrong thing when there is so much opposition. Many men told me I was out of place and God would never call a woman to work with boys in gangs and prisons. I was not allowed seats at the table to share my expertise and knowledge of all the years of experience I had simply because I was a woman.

UNTIL GOD SHOWS YOU YOUR WHAT, JUST KEEP LOVING GOD, LOVING PEOPLE, SHARING JESUS.

So why did I keep pursuing it? Because I *knew* that's what God called me to—and until the very same men who opposed me came to my block and loved on my boys, I wasn't going to stop. Positive men were not present on my block, so was I not supposed to be out there trying? Just know, when you *know*, you won't let anything keep you from what God has ordained you to do or the people he strategically has you meet to show others hope, light, and love.

Be prepared that the way God uses you won't be exactly the way you had planned. At the time I lived in Humboldt Park with my boys from the block, I knew I had to create activities for them to do to keep them safe and off the street at peak hours. I have always believed that youth will tell you what they want and that is the best way to keep them engaged and have ownership over an activity or program. I remember gathering the boys together on the block and asking them what their interests were, what they liked to do.

"I'm all about hip-hop culture," I said excitedly. "I can have DJ classes, breakdance classes, graffiti classes. You name it, I know someone." I just knew they would be excited to explore the hip-hop world. After all, they were urban teenagers!

"Well, Miss Amy," said Jose. "All we really like to do is play basketball and smoke weed."

Dang it! That's not what I wanted to hear.

"Well, I can definitely help you with one of those," I said. "But the other one? You on your own with that!"

I went home deflated. Not for the reason you may be thinking, though. Basketball was my *past* life. After my husband left, I didn't want anything to do with basketball. I didn't want to watch it, own one, or go to a game. I was done with that life. But God said not so. The very thing that caused issues in my marriage was now the way to connect with the boys on the block? God, you got jokes. I started a basketball team.

YES TO MY CALLING

I'll never forget the day I fully embraced my calling when I was in my thirties. Everything was going amazing for me at the Orlando DeVos Urban Leadership Initiative conference, until the news of our evening event was announced. Tickets to the Orlando Magic basketball game, along with a locker room tour. Sounds great for most, but it was triggering for me. I had just left behind the basketball world, and I knew a couple of Magic players at the time. I sat in my seat and tears started to well up. I had no idea it would impact me this much. I wrestled with going or not. How could I sit there for hours being triggered the whole time? I couldn't. I told my regional director (she wasn't too happy with me), but I knew it was not healthy for me to be there. No one really understood, but I had to fight for my well-being.

My cohort leader at the time was asked to persuade me to attend. She pulled me to the side after everyone left. I was fighting a flood of tears choking my throat. I knew she was going to demand that I go, and I didn't know how I was going to do it.

We sat down and she patiently listened to my story. The story of the life I was trying to disconnect from, to heal from, to start fresh from. I cried as I talked.

"I've always felt like Robert was the one called to youth ministry and I was just a helper," I explained. "He was the one chosen and now here I am, still doing youth ministry without him."

"Maybe it's because *you* were the one who was really called," Teresa said gently as she held my hand. "The Scripture says, 'He will separate the wheat from the chaff and clear the rubbish.' He clearly has the one he called still doing ministry."

The tears seemed to dry up instantly. I looked her straight in her eyes as if an angel had just given me divine revelation. *I* was the one called to ministry. God was preparing *me*! I felt this to the core of my soul. In that moment, no matter what anyone said, no matter the challenges I was facing, no matter the people who were against me, I walked into my calling with full confidence. After that conversation, no one could challenge my calling without a fight. This was what I was made for, and I fully embraced it that day. The world was in trouble now.

And I didn't go to the game.

SEVENTEEN

THE GIFT OF BROKENNESS

The sacrifices of God are a broken spirit;
a broken and contrite heart, O God, you will not despise.

Psalm 51:17

I lost the most important man in my life, my daddy, on December 13, 2022.

I also lost my "most bestest" friend in my life of thirty-one years, Tiwanda, on June 2, 2023.

Both to cancer.

I am in a cloud of darkness, sorrow, anger, and pain, and I feel like I can't breathe. Smack dab in the middle (front, back, and every side) of brokenness. My heart and soul are shattered into a trillion pieces, pieces that can't fit back together.

I've had a lot of loss in my life, but I've never lost a parent. It's an unfathomable emptiness and pain I've never endured. I was a daddy's girl, always will be. He was my foundation, my superhero, the first man I loved. He was one of a kind. I could go on and on about my dad. But without him, I find myself in a new space with God, with my life.

Then to lose my best friend five months later is a new wound on top of an already open wound. Eighty-one days after she told me the news, she was gone. Tiwanda kept me a Christian on many occasions and always pointed me to God. Her laughter healed my soul more times than I can count.

I am devastated and brokenhearted, the kind of brokenness there seems to be no healing for. But God will show me differently. The Scripture reminds us that "the LORD is near to the brokenhearted" (Psalm 34:18). If this is true, he's never been closer to me than he is right now because my heart has never been so broken. Hear my prayer, Lord.

Brokenness, a state of emotional pain that stops someone from living a normal or healthy life, can switch the direction of your life in a moment. When we feel broken, it usually looks like hopelessness or despair. It can look like a broken heart or a broken spirit. Sometimes it comes through as low self-esteem or feeling unworthy to be loved.

When I was previously at my most broken (during my divorce and the loss of my niece in 2001), I found I leaned more heavily on God. I had to bring my broken heart to the altar. I had to recognize that the only way I would get through this season and be healed was by God. The only way I could walk was if God put his hands on my legs like a puppet and moved them.

And he did. Daily. One foot in front of the other. In all my years, I had never been closer to God than I was then. I learned more about God and myself than at any other time in my life. He showed me his faithfulness, something I had always doubted (in both man and God).

Brokenness comes in many forms for different people. No one can escape it, but the one thing all broken people have in common is that we don't have to stay that way.

> **THE ONE THING ALL BROKEN PEOPLE HAVE IN COMMON IS THAT WE DON'T HAVE TO STAY THAT WAY.**

But now, O LORD, you are our Father;

we are the clay, and you are our potter;

we are all the work of your hand. (Isaiah 64:8)

GOD USES OUR PAIN

My pain prepared me for my ministry journey.

As a teenager, when my brother was lost to the streets and prison, I felt helpless. I didn't have the capacity or resources to help pull him out of the darkness. But now, as an adult, I can help others. I can help those who, like my brother, don't have the help they need to change the trajectory of their lives. When I look at every gang member, every incarcerated individual, I see my baby brother. I see young men who are brilliant, talented, and lovable. I see young men and women who have stories, usually of trauma, abandonment, and pain. I see young boys and girls who are good people experiencing tough circumstances and lack of access to resources. I see families that are impacted by gang membership or incarceration. I see communities that suffer as a result. Like the dad in the movie *Freedom Writers* said to his daughter Erin, "You, my dear, have been blessed with a burden." I know the stories. I was the story. But now, I can help.

God is a God who never wastes our pain or hurt. Romans 8:28 reminds us that "all things work together for good, for those who are called according to his purpose." We are wounded healers helping heal the wounded. But why would God choose to use our deepest hurts to shape our ministry? It almost seems like suffering is a prerequisite to an impactful ministry. What is the gain for pain? How can we use it to impact the lives of others as we walk with those who are in vulnerable spaces?

Here is how God uses our pain and healing:

To develop our compassion for others. The Bible calls God the Father of compassion, and we are to model him. In 1 Peter 3:8 he calls us to "be like-minded, be sympathetic, love one another, be compassionate and humble" (NIV). Compassion is a connector of hearts and stories. The more we hear and understand stories, the stronger our compassion muscle becomes. Even in our own pain, we long for compassion from God and others, and by receiving compassion, we can offer it to others. The heart of compassion longs for action. You can't have compassion for someone without wanting to help or do something.

To strengthen connections with others. When you meet someone where they are in their pain journey, you become an ally to them. You may have a shared commonality with someone who seeks you for understanding. Sharing your struggle brings you closer together and strengthens your connection. We discover our need for each other as we navigate our struggles. Ecclesiastes 4:9 reminds us, "Two are better than one, because they have a good reward for their toil." Stronger connections build stronger communities.

To comfort others. You've been where others are—and you remember how it felt. You remember the need to be comforted, the need to be heard. We serve a God of comfort, and he "comforts us in all our affliction, so that we may be able to comfort those who are in any affliction, with the comfort with which we ourselves are comforted by God" (2 Corinthians 1:4). We are also to "rejoice with those who rejoice; weep with those who weep" (Romans 12:15). Sometimes just sitting with someone in their pain is all they require. Your presence is a comfort. Comforting others validates their pain and says, "In your hurt, I see you."

To show others God can heal. As the saying goes, "Hurt people hurt people." But I also believe, "Healed people help others heal." Our healing journey can be an example of God's power to heal them too. Whether we are seeking physical, emotional, or spiritual healing, God is in the business of renewing us. We become a walking billboard for Jehovah Rafa (the God who heals). The testimony of healing gives people hope and points them toward Christ:

> He was pierced for our transgressions;
>> he was crushed for our iniquities;
> upon him was the chastisement that brought us peace,
>> and with his wounds we are healed. (Isaiah 53:5)

Helen Keller once said, "Although the world is full of suffering, it is full also of the overcoming of it."

God uses our pain, but what if we also saw pain as a gift? A gift and an opportunity for growth, especially in our ministry? God can use our pain to develop us and push us out of our comfort zone. And if you're like me, you often need pushing. It is in times when pain challenges us to grow that we see our inner strength and total need to depend on God.

The pain of competing with the streets for my brother brought me closer to God. I learned to trust God with what was most valuable to me. It pushed me to be honest with myself about my need for a God who cared for my brother and could take care of my brother more than I ever could.

> IT IS IN TIMES WHEN PAIN CHALLENGES US TO GROW THAT WE SEE OUR INNER STRENGTH AND TOTAL NEED TO DEPEND ON GOD.

And because of my experiences, I can connect with others who are in the same place I used to be. I understand the fear, the worry, the helplessness. I can comfort those who have lost loved ones to gun violence because, I too, have lost many young people I loved. I have strong relationships with those who have had or currently have someone they love in prison because I do too. We cry together. We laugh together. We struggle together. Your pain has value.

■ ▪ ■

Chuckie was sitting alone in the teen center at the prison. I walked over to him and started a conversation. He became vulnerable and shared about his mom.

"She doesn't even love me; she doesn't want me," he said, fighting the tears. "Don't know my dad. I just don't care about anything. That's why I'm here. Why would anyone want me?"

Many of my young people truly believe they are broken to the point of worthlessness and uselessness. They don't think in big terms, like being used by God, but simply that God doesn't see any worth in them. They have no chance, and they are in straight survival mode.

Though we may not see our worth through our woundedness, being broken in the hands of God allows the Creator to shape us into his image, his dream for us. We are not scattered pieces like a broken Christmas bulb that falls loudly from the tree branch with no more worth to God. He doesn't throw us away. He gathers the pieces and gently begins to heal us. Like Bryan Stevenson shares, each of us is more than the worst thing we've ever done.[1]

I have an exercise I do every year with the Bishop McNamara High School students during Senior Day. I hand out glow sticks to every student to hold.

"What do you hold in your hand?" I ask.

"Glow stick," they yell back.

"In its original form, is it doing what it's supposed to do?" I ask.

"No!" they scream.

"What's its purpose?"

"To shine light," a few students yell.

"But what you have now does not shine light. So how do we get it to work?"

"Break it!" They yell.

"Then break it," I screamed.

We turn the lights off and the room glows with pink, purple, yellow, and orange lights.

"And this is like us," I say. "We can shine brightly even in our brokenness. You think you need to have it all together, but even in your brokenness, there is light! He pulls you out of darkness because you are light."

WOUNDED HEALERS

For years I refused to talk about my divorce. I relocated to Chicago and never let anyone know I failed at my marriage and it ended in divorce. Christians I encountered often judged me for it and made me feel shame for the failure—without even knowing all the details. Church and divorce bring shame, judgment, and embarrassment. For all these reasons and more, I hid my brokenness. I didn't talk about my experience of abandonment, mental abuse, and, ultimately, the ending of my marriage. It wasn't until a year later that I saw a friend at the beginning of her divorce journey suffering the same treatment I had received. I reached out to her—and I walked through it with her. I became a wounded healer.

Wounded healers allow us to use our own woundedness to bring healing to others. Wounded healers are those whose painful experiences can be used to help others in their journey of healing. Our wounds become a source of healing for others. Henri Nouwen shares in *The Wounded Healer*, "When we become aware that we do not have to escape our pains, but that we can mobilize them into a common search for life, those very pains are transformed from expressions of despair into signs of hope. . . . This is so because a shared pain is no longer paralyzing but mobilizing, when understood as a way to liberation."[2]

We can decide that our brokenness is in fact a gift that blesses others as they battle their own woundedness. We no longer look at our brokenness as a shame but as a tool to be used for the greater good of the kingdom. Something God can use to further the work of growth and showing others he is the God that heals. God's wounded healer was Jesus, who was wounded so we could be healed. "But it was our sins that did that to him, that ripped and tore and crushed him—*our sins*! He took the punishment, and that made us whole. Through his bruises we get healed" (Isaiah 53:5 MSG). We have the ultimate wounded healer to follow as an example of how our brokenness can impact generations and change lives.

I have had the privilege of walking with women going through divorce, helping them to not feel like a failure or of no value. Others who have lost their dad have walked with me through my loss and helped me to grieve—and I will be able to do that for others in the future.

Look at your pain and wounds as part of the human condition, not as an individualistic punishment, curse, or destiny. See the power and blessing of how your wounds can help to heal others. In spite of the fact that I'm broken, God uses me. This is the gift of brokenness.

PART CUATRO

SEEING HOPE

EIGHTEEN

BUILDING TOGETHER THROUGH TEACHABLE MOMENTS

If you want to go fast, go alone. If you want to go far, go together.

Aᴏꜰꜰᴀᴄ Pʀᴏᴠᴇʀʙ

"My life should have been over," Luis said passionately. "Over the last fifteen years, I ducked fifteen years in the feds and had my OG's crib shot up (if it wasn't for the couch, I woulda got shot more than two times)."

It was at this time that Luis's family moved from the block and I lost contact with him. I had heard many things through the "gang grapevine" but could never track Luis down. I had

heard about the attempt on his life and about his best friend being killed.

"The day my best friend was killed, I was supposed to be with him, but my baby momma dragged me to church. I went into a dark place and did things I shouldn't have and I caught this case I have now. This is when I found faith in God. I was facing five attempted murder charges with a minimum of twenty-five years. Through the grace of God, my lawyer got my case down to nine years at 85 percent" (which means Luis must serve 85 percent of his sentence).

"On this journey, I asked God for a sign for guidance," Luis said. "One day I was laying in my bunk watching TV and mail was getting passed out. I heard my name being called and was surprised. It was a card. When I seen who it was from, I had the biggest smile on my face. The *last* person I thought I would hear from! It was Amy.

"Little did I know my prayer had been answered. God sent his angel back into my life to finish the work he started years ago. I thank him each day for answering my prayers cuz he not only gave me a mentor, he gave me a big sister, family, someone I can always count on. I wish I would have never lost contact with her or hid from her cuz I would have became a different person. My life would have changed a long time ago."

Sitting in the lobby of Cook County Division 11 waiting to visit one of my youth, I looked around and saw pain in the faces, words, and postures of those waiting to see someone who was in even more pain than we were. I not only saw it, I felt it in my spirit and aching heart.

Actually, this week was full of pain. I was surrounded by hurting people who have no escape from the pain that engulfs them, pain that has become a comfort zone, that has simply paralyzed them from seeing possibility and opportunity. Sometimes the pain is so great it's like driving on a highway on a foggy day with zero visibility so that you can't see the car directly in front of you.

This week alone, I held a very depressed young man who cried in my arms as he was awaiting his fate for his court case.

I talked on the phone with a beautiful young lady who is in so much pain she has rebelled against everything she believes in and feels lost in this world.

I had a one-sided conversation with someone who is desperately trying to push me away because it's the only way he knows to protect his heart and feel safe in the world—by not letting anyone get too close.

I sat behind a thick prison glass window with a youth who experienced joy in seeing me, but tears came when he knew our time was coming to an end and he felt the pain of not being able to get a hug—which he had desperately longed for for nine months.

This week alone, I learned the power of four little words that brought tears to the eyes of at least three of those in the above situations: *You are not alone.*

There is something about these words that releases the pain being held in the hearts of people. Pain that is being protected like an heirloom in a safety deposit box, like a car alarm on a brand-new Benz. Pain is a comfort zone for many people, and for many people it's all they know. I see many young people who truly have accepted that without pain in their day-to-day life, something is out of order. So they sabotage a perfectly wonderful day or relationship in order to feel "normal."

But I have seen these four little words allow someone to put down their guard, if only for a minute, to allow the pain to be released and become vulnerable—even trusting—in the arms of the one who utters these words of comfort.

Poet Maya Angelou shares, "No one, but no one can make it out here alone."[1] Even the Word of God says, "If they fall, one will lift up his fellow. But woe to him who is alone when he falls and has not another to lift him up!" (Ecclesiastes 4:10). We were not created to be alone but to be in community, to be together. But somehow the enemy has convinced many of us that we are alone.

Telling someone they are not alone reassures them they are cared for, that someone is concerned about what happens to them, and that there is a genuine commitment to walk with them through their pain. It doesn't mean you have the answer to their problems or a miracle pill to make it better. It simply means, "I will not abandon you. We are in this together."

I had the privilege of becoming good friends with a high-ranking gang leader in Chicago. We'll call him Chief. We actually met on Facebook through a mutual friend in California. He introduced us through Messenger and we began sharing our lives. Our mutual friend really cared about this man and wanted desperately for him to know the love and freedom of Christ. My goal was different. I just wanted to know and learn from him, see where he was in this world, and offer support and kindness. The Jesus part would then come naturally.

Chief's family was full of Christians, pastors, and so on, but his history with the church has been one of hurt and distrust. As a gang leader he has had a few relationships with pastors who have made promises to him and his boys, but they never followed through "until there were news cameras around," he would say. "Then they would reach out and ask me to be there with them."

One day Chief gave his life to Christ and denounced his gang leadership. A pastor took him under his wing but immediately put him on a speaking circuit. He was speaking all over the country, in magazines, on TV shows, at churches. He was thrown into the Christian-speaking world without discipleship or mentorship. Many pastors surrounded him, but Chief said it was as if the pastors cared more about exploiting him than caring for his soul, his pain, his trauma, and his need for healing. He felt used by them.

What's more, being a Christian didn't change the fact that he had been a well-known gang leader, and he was still dabbling in that world. Chief was shot (believed to be organized by a pastor) and ended up spending months in the hospital fighting for his life. He was also going through a divorce at the time and didn't feel supported.

"When I was in the hospital, none of those pastors called me or visited," Chief said. I could see the hurt in his eyes. "Guess who came to visit me? The boys, my old crew. That's when I made the decision to leave Christianity and go back to the gang." They welcomed him back with open arms.

And then here I come years later! Of course, it was a slow-building process as trust is hard for him to give. He was cautious with me, but because of his relationship with our mutual friend, he was willing to give me a shot. Over that year we became good friends. He invited me to spend Easter with his family and I couldn't refuse. It was a blessing to meet his parents and his children. We hung out in the backyard listening to music, laughing, sharing, and eating Puerto Rican cuisine. It was like being with family. Many people were against me hanging out with Chief, but I knew the friendship we had developed, the connection we had, and how God had ordained it. Chief would never let anything happen to me and I always felt protected.

One day we were hanging out at his house on the porch. Many young gang members were coming by, speaking, doing what they needed to do, and one of the youth was on his way to work. He talked about how he needed to make enough money to buy his kids school supplies and clothes. After he left, Chief explained this is a challenge for a lot of his guys. They struggle to provide for their kids. I understood and my heart was saddened.

I posted something on Facebook about how my heart had been challenged and I wished there was something I could do. A friend, Mark, who ran a large youth ministry organization, reached out and said, "I believe we can help!" He proceeded to donate hundreds of bookbags with school supplies inside to hand out on the corner. The day the packages arrived, I hugged the boxes and cried over them.

The next week Chief, his daughter, my friend Carmen, and I set up shop on the corner near Chief's house. We had bookbags, Bibles, and hugs ready. He sent out a message to all his boys to bring their kids and come grab some supplies. Some of the fellas brought water and snacks to pass out. Chief said this had never been done before and it was a big deal to them. The community didn't know what was going on but the joy of seeing families in need smiling brought me more joy than my heart could handle. Watching Chief hand out the supplies, talk with families, and laugh made me see even more the humanity of this man many deem a monster. It seemed to be a contradiction considering his gang leadership role, but today I saw a man who truly cared about people.

I posted about this event on Facebook, sharing pictures and describing the joy of the day. I got several mean messages saying as a Christian, how dare I hang out with a gang leader who is destroying our communities with drugs, guns, and violence? How dare I let him help me give to his members who are also destroying the city? How was I really helping anyone by giving them just a bookbag and a Bible? I couldn't believe our goodwill and intentions were being criticized by these people— people I thought understood the mission. But I also understood that not everyone would get it. An impact was made not only in the community but in the heart of a gang leader and his members.

Jesus was a fan of teachable moments, unplanned opportunities that can be taken advantage of for learning. Some people learn best this way instead of a direct lesson. Because teachable moments are often spontaneous, we must be on the lookout for them. Teachable moments teach others how to think and can challenge their worldviews.

All my life I have driven a manual five-speed vehicle. I was taught how to drive using one. I loved being a woman who drove a five-speed—it was a rare sight. One afternoon on Beach Ave, my youth were gassing me up because I was a woman with a manual drive. I asked them if they knew how to drive one. They all backed up from the car laughing.

"Well, do you want to learn how?"

They all jumped at the idea. One youth said it was a dream of his to own a five-speed car that he could drive. This was the time. So every Sunday afternoon, I took three youth to Humboldt Park where there wasn't a lot of traffic. Nothing like seeing hardcore boys freaking out behind the wheel of a car. They were scared, nervous, excited. I felt the same.

One afternoon I took the youth to the south side of the park. We were still working on the basics. It was always funny to see them decide who was going first. No one ever volunteered. On this day, Mikey took the wheel. We were going to learn how to reverse.

We came to the end of the road where the yellow gates they use to close the park were open to the side. We needed to turn around, but the turnaround would require reversing. Mikey was going to try it. He started to slowly turn and lost control of the car. It went forward and hit the yellow gate. The boys in the back were laughing and cracking jokes on Mikey. Mikey was embarrassed and apologetic. We all jumped out of the car and saw the yellow paint from the gate smeared on my dark green Acura.

"Miss Amy, I am so sorry," he exclaimed. "I will pay to get it fixed. I promise."

The boys were still laughing and teasing Mikey.

"Are you hurt?" I asked. "Everyone okay?"

"Yeah, we're good," they all proclaimed.

"Look, Mikey," I said. "It's just a car. It's really not a big deal. Just a piece of metal. As long as you're okay, we're good."

"But we need to fix it," he sighed. "It's an Acura. You can't drive around with that on it."

"Actually, if you don't mind, I'd like to leave it there as a memory," I said. "Will make me smile every time I see it."

Mikey and the boys looked at me like I was crazy, but soon we were all laughing, including Mikey. That day the lesson continued.

It was a teachable moment. All I wanted them to know was they were more valuable than that car, that things don't matter as much as their safety, and that life is about creating memories.

And every time I drove through the block, the boys would check to see if it was still there—and we would laugh. Every time.

I usually get a lot of young people hitting on me. It's quite hilarious because they could be my children, but it happens. It is easy to shut them down, but I try to use those incidents as teachable moments.

One afternoon I was slowly riding through the block on Beach Ave. One of the boys saw me coming from the stoop where five of his friends were sitting smoking and drinking.

"Hold up, Miss Amy," he yelled as he ran to the street. I pulled over to the side and parked my car.

"What's good, Gabriel?"

"Nothing much," he states. "You know my birthday is coming up. I'm about to be eighteen." He winks at me and looks back at his boys so they can gas him up.

"Well, congrats," I said. "That's a great age."

"Yeah, so I was thinking," he said smoothly. "Since I'm about to be legal, can I take you out?"

Don't laugh, Amy. Don't look shocked. Just stay cool. Use this moment.

"Um, yeah, okay," I smiled coyly. "I'll go out with you if you can answer a couple of questions for me."

"No doubt!" he exclaimed, looking back at his boys again for approval.

"Okay, first question," I said, setting him up. "What time are you picking me up? Oh wait, you don't have a car. Okay, no problem, I'll drive.

"What restaurant are we going to? And remember, I ain't no McDonald's kinda girl. You gotta take me to Cheesecake Factory or Grand Lux Cafe," I said boldly. "Oh wait, you don't have a job. That's okay, I'll pay this one time.

"What are we going to do afterward? We going back to your crib?" I questioned. "Oh wait, you live with your mom. She would probably have to hang out with us too, huh?"

He stood there silent.

"Look, papa," I said gently. "I am flattered, I am. But it takes a lot to be with a woman like me. I have high expectations. So why don't we just remain friends and I won't tell a soul."

"Okay, Miss Amy," Gabriel said humbly. "I gotcha."

The next day, as I was sitting on my stoop, Gabriel walked to the gate.

"Hey, Miss Amy!" he said. "Can I ask you a question?"

"Of course you can," I exclaimed. "Come on in and sit with me. What's up?"

"Well, I was wondering," he said inquisitively, "What *does* it take to get a woman like you?"

And we sat for hours talking about that: relationships and Cheesecake Factory cheesecake.

Over lunch Chief and I were having a discussion about the church. I asked him if there was a message he wanted to share with and about the church in my book.

"For every action, there is a reaction—good or bad, there's a reaction," he said.

At first I didn't understand where he was going with this. Then he reminded me of an "action" we tried together and now the "reaction" has been increased community violence in a certain neighborhood.

There was a church that had opened up down the block from Chief's home and the blocks where his boys were set up. They had a couple of parking lots (a rare thing in Chicago) and I would dream of what we could use them for to keep kids safe and off the streets (basketball games, volleyball, cookouts, outdoor movies . . .). I would talk to Chief about it, and he was down to help keep the church "off-limits" to protect the youth and families there.

I was close friends with the senior pastor, and he let me know they wanted to reach out to the community and impact those involved in gangs and help alleviate the gang violence in that neighborhood. The person he had selected to lead this endeavor was a young man who was a former gang member himself and had just come home from a stint in prison but was new to ministry. The pastor asked me to meet with him. Of course I would! I was excited at what this could mean for Chief and his boys. This could mean resources, healing, and saved lives.

I was excited to meet with this young man, but very quickly, he shut me down. He didn't want to hear anything I had to say. He thought he knew how to do this because he was from the streets and I wasn't. What I had to offer (the relationships, outreach ideas) wasn't part of his strategy. I can't be of help to someone who doesn't see a need for partnership. I called the pastor and shared how the meeting went. He asked me to please not give up. He asked me if I could help them figure out what gang sets were around the church so they could begin to know the neighborhood and create a strategy.

No one knows these blocks better than Chief, so I reached out to him. He was hesitant to help the church, but because of our relationship, he was willing to help me—knowing I only wanted to help his boys and the other youth too. We jumped into his car and he took me on a tour of all the blocks surrounding the church. I wrote down all the gang corners on a map: history, names, and so on.

I was excited to go back to the pastor and the ministry leader with this information. Chief even agreed to meet with them and me. Crickets. I never heard back from them.

"For every action, there is a reaction—good or bad, there's a reaction," Chief said calmly. "We tried to help and they ignored us. Now look at all the violence and gang activity happening around that church area. We could have changed that. Y'all want me to trust the church? I'm still mad about that one.

"The church comes with promises and we're like, yeah yeah yeah, we've heard that before," Chief continued. "When will the church be about their word? I just don't trust them."

I understand his trauma. I understand his worldview. The church can sometimes be a dysfunctional family. Though the church has caused a lot of hurt, we are also the place where healing can happen if we're open, intentional, and willing to do what others won't. Intention means nothing without action. Chief is in need of healing and the church should be the first place (and the safe space) to do so.

The church had a great opportunity to build together. They missed it. Don't miss the chance to build together because the plan, the tools, the person might not come in the package you were expecting. God's work has no boundaries. You can't put the work of God in a box. Build with what you have, with what God sends you—and change your community for the better.

Luis and his friends had been running the block all day. They were tired, hungry, and high—and they were craving my brownies.

All the youth on the block knew Miss Amy kept brownies at her house in case any of them ever wanted some. On this day they decided to stop and grab some. I came to the door, and they were begging for some.

"I don't have any," I apologized. "But if you come back in about an hour, I will make some for you."

"That's cool," Luis said. "We'll just wait right here."

And they waited. For an hour. On my porch.

They ate the whole pan of brownies until they were sick. We sat and talked for hours.

Relationship building can be done even over a pan of warm chocolate brownies.

Building relationships with high-risk youth is a process that requires great commitment. Building together with high-risk youth is a privilege that requires great humbleness. The only way to do this is to make sure young people have a place at the table. That they are heard, seen, and valued. I would never think of building a youth ministry without youth as the leadership guiding and steering the ship. Our job is to train ourselves out of a job. We are building leaders who can take over when our stint in ministry is done—or even before.

Many believe that children are the future. I believe they are the *now* as well. When building with those on the margins, it is important to recognize and acknowledge that they are part of the solution; they are their own heroes. Many say that we must stand on behalf of the voiceless. I truly believe people aren't voiceless. I believe we're just not listening.

Building together is just that—we are *together* while learning.

NINETEEN

DEATH ALMOST KILLED ME

How lucky I am to have something that makes saying goodbye so hard.

A. A. MILNE, *WINNIE THE POOH*

It never occurred to me that intervention work meant I would lose many of the young people I loved to gun violence. No one prepared me for the intense heartbreak I would experience by burying my young people month after month, year after year. I always wonder, if I did know, would I have still chosen to walk in this calling?

Senseless loss after loss. Too many funerals. Too many families in pain. Communities impacted by the loss. My own heart was torn into pieces—and I had to keep going. Had to keep loving young people hard, even at the risk of losing them, too. I

stayed in a constant state of grief for a while. The weight of carrying the grief impacted how I did ministry and how I viewed every youth I encountered. It almost killed me.

◼ ◼ ◼

Jonathan Sanchez's life journey was full of trauma, pain, and hopelessness. Physical abuse. Gang membership. Drug abuse. Molestation. Guns. Abandonment. Foster care. Prison (for half his life).

Jonathan's story is unique yet also common among those who join gangs or spend time in prisons. Trauma is a part of their story. Trying to survive it is too.

Jonathan and I met through his girlfriend's sister, Krystle. She reached out to me on Facebook and a friendship between us quickly began. For years Krystle did not like Jonathan, but she worked through her feelings and forgave him for his past and the hurt he had caused. She quickly became his biggest advocate and friend.

In 2014, Jonathan was going to be coming home from prison. Krystle wanted to help him walk into a better life than the one he had been living—and he was ready. She was able to find a transitional home for him in Chicago, which allowed him to be released earlier.

While at the home, Jonathan had some tattoos on his hands and arms he wanted removed, and I knew exactly where to take him. It was our first time meeting. I asked Jonathan many questions that day, including why he wanted his tattoos removed.

"When I'm walking down the street, holding my son's hand, I don't want anything to keep me from being able to do that," he said. "If someone sees my gang affiliation, they could start shooting, and I'm not putting my kid at risk." That day the tattoos were removed.

I took him to Chick-fil-A for the first time. He enjoyed his salad as I asked him questions. He loved talking about his son. I asked him how he was sure he was ready to change his life. His answer changed me.

"Because I don't have the right to die anymore," he said. "My son needs me."

I use that line now for every gang-involved young person I come across who is a parent.

When I asked Jonathan what he thought of me when we first met, he said, "I thought you were crazy . . . and different. But that's why I wanted to hang out with you." And we never stopped hanging out.

Jonathan was one of the most talented young men I have ever met. He could do everything from cooking amazing dishes to writing stories and poetry to being an amazing dad (his biggest passion). He and I clicked and became close. I saw gifts in him, and he wanted to change the world, beginning with his gang brothers and those in prison. The goal was to mentor and train him to be a mentor and a speaker/trainer. We were able to do a couple of videos together (check out www.ahopedealer.org /videos) and had a few speaking engagements lined up. He was murdered two days before our first one.

This is Jonathan's story, in Jonathan's words. It was Jonathan's dream that the world hear and be impacted by his life and story, just as I was. I introduce you to my Jonathan:[1]

INTERVIEWER: Tell me a little bit about your family.

JONATHAN: Well, altogether I got five brothers, six sisters. I'm the third youngest from my dad and the second youngest from my mom and growin' up it was just me and my two other brothers. I was on and off with my dad and my sisters. All my sisters lived with my dad, so I used to go over there and hang out but my mom she was strung out on drugs at the time. My dad, he was into the streets, gangbanging. I was left out alone.

At the age of eight, my mom got so strung out on drugs that she got me and my two brothers tooken away by [the Illinois Department of Children and Family Services]. They gave me and my older brother an option because my other brother is disabled. They like, one of y'all gotta stick with him. At the time I just told my brother, look you go 'head I'll be cool. So I was in foster care for three years. On and off I ran away from home.

My dad didn't really care about us. My family didn't really care about me at the time cuz they was too much worried about my little brother and my older brother. So I was just left out on the tracks. The only thing I had, my only option, was the streets to survive so I could eat and have clothes on my back.

INTERVIEWER: How did it make you feel at the time, when it seemed like nobody cared about you?

JONATHAN: I felt lonely, depressed, ashamed, lost, all of the above. It's what caused me to have all this pain, all this anger. Me, I was to the point where I would lash out on other people. That's why when I was in a gang, I was wonderin' whose ruthless guys were around. Cuz at the time when the guys came and say, "Yo it's time for war," I'm right there in front of everybody [saying], "Let's go. I'm cocked and loaded. Let's go, I'm ready to ride." It's just that loneliness I had. The streets was the only thing there that gave me an opening, made me feel like I was wanted at the time.

INTERVIEWER: So when you were in the front of the line when there was something going on, did you have fear? Or was it like you didn't care that much?

JONATHAN: I didn't really care as much cuz I looked at it like this—ain't nobody care for me so why should I care for myself? At the time I had nothin' to worry about. I had no kid at the time, my mom strung out on drugs, didn't care about me cuz if she did I woulda never went to the foster home. So basically, it was like I was fearless and careless. I didn't care what another person felt, what they thought about me.

INTERVIEWER: So when you're growing up and you're young and no one wants you and you're in a foster home, what was it like trying to make a connection with another human being? When did you first learn to care about someone else?

JONATHAN: It took me many years to feel the way I feel right now, how I feel with my girlfriend and my son. It took me many years of a lot of hatred built in me, a lot of ashamedness, and a lot of being lost in life.

I spent nine years of my life locked up, not mentally stable, where I didn't have a person to write me, a person to come visit me, or a person to even give me a letter to keep my head up, keep going, we're here for you, none of that. So all that hatred I had when I was a kid, when it led me to jail—all that time it just built up so bad. When I came home in 2014 from doin' my nine years it was still there. Then once I met my girlfriend in 2015, she kept tellin' me to do certain things and tried to get me outta my element. Even when I got shot in 2015, I got shot six times and left for dead on the sidewalk, she found out I was in the hospital. She was the first person at the side of my bed waitin' on me to wake up, wake up out of my coma. And ever since then we just like, I felt like somebody actually cared about me, somebody really loves me.

INTERVIEWER: Do you remember when you first were aware of the negativity of the street?

JONATHAN: Well I used to have a sister. She used to go out with gang members. I used to watch them hang out in front of the cars, throw bottles, bricks, and I used to realize like, what are they doing? One of my older brothers took me out one day and was showing me the streets and trying to teach me how to survive and how to keep my head straight. He showed me my first gun, [how to] hold it. Around the age of eight or nine he used to tell me, man, do the gettin' but don't get got. What he meant by that: make sure you're the one behind the gun. Don't let them swipe you; don't be in front of the gun.

INTERVIEWER: When was the first time you shot the gun?

JONATHAN: I shot a gun my first time when I was like ten years old. We was hanging out in the backyard. My brother had brung it out and said, man, look. I didn't know what it was, I grabbed the gun like a toy and I shot it. It went off and hit the garage. And ever since then I got the thrill of hearing the noise and having that power in my hands. It just made me turn into the person I was behind that mask.

INTERVIEWER: Have you ever shot at someone else?

JONATHAN: Several times.

INTERVIEWER: When was the first time?

JONATHAN: When I was eleven years old, I used to hang out with some guys and I was the smallest guy in the crowd, the fastest. So every time we walked around, they'd hand me the gun. "Here, come walk around with us." A'ight cool. And one day we were walking around, a car full of guys came and pulled up on us ready to jump out on us, fight with us. I pulled the gun out and started firing. A couple hours later, I got arrested for discharge of a firearm.

INTERVIEWER: What was your charge when you got sent to prison?

JONATHAN: At the age of fifteen I was charged with two counts of attempted murder, attempt to kill with two firearms. I was facing thirty to sixty years and my first offer was forty-five years at the door, and they said that was the minimum they were going for. I fought that case for almost three years and they finally came down ten years. I pleaded guilty; I did my time.

In the process my mom was cleaning her act up, getting off drugs. She was doing good. I was like four and a half years in and she was proud; she was like, man, you're coming home in four years. I'm happy that you're coming home already, see how fast time flyin'? So I said all right.

That same week, the day before she died, I talked to her. She was like, man, I'm going to the hospital. I'm not feeling too good. I said all right I'll call you tomorrow ma, I love you. If you need anything just call down here and let me know to call you when you get out the hospital.

I didn't get a call from her the next day. So I went to the phone and I dialed her number and my little brother picked up hysterical and was like, mom is dying, mom is dying. I was like what, what you talking about, look hold on. He put my aunt on the phone and she was like, your mom's dying, she's not gonna make it. She got the swine flu, she not gonna make it.

All I remember was I was on the phone, I broke down got on my knees and just started crying in front of the whole game room. Everybody that was at that table playing cards, they just stopped and looked at me. I was just right there sitting on the floor next to the phone just bawling in tears.

INTERVIEWER: How did you learn how to say I love you to your mom and other people and show interest in them?

JONATHAN: Well, I started saying I love you to my mom when she started cleaning her act up with the drugs. When she was off drugs she was a totally different person, she was outgoing, understanding. She wasn't judging me for the mistakes I made in life. So I used to tell her I love her all the time and we just started communicating again. She'd come visit me once I moved units. That same week she died I was supposed to get a visit from her, and just in the blink of an eye she was just gone. That quick.

INTERVIEWER: Was it when your mother died that the mask fell off?

JONATHAN: My mother died and it was like my mask was loose. It was somewhat getting ready to come off, but once she died, that mask went on super tight and all my hatred and pain built up even more. That mask was basically crazy glued onto my face. It was just . . . I went crazy. I came home from the penitentiary in 2014 and I just went crazy. I started drinking a lot, started running the streets again, playing with guns, chasing people, beating up people. I just lost it, I lost my mind.

INTERVIEWER: Did you have a feeling that you wanted to inflict your pain on others?

JONATHAN: I felt like that. I felt like if I can't be happy with my parent, with my mother that cared for me, why should I let others feel the joy of having someone around? So I used to cause pain against a lot of people and hurt a lot of people.

INTERVIEWER: You had just gotten out of jail after nine years, yet you went crazy and started doing a lot of bad things. Were you worried about going back to jail for a long time?

JONATHAN: I was worried a little bit cuz I didn't really have much to lose. But once my girl told me she was pregnant, I started calming down a lot . . . and being shot at the same time calmed me down. So I was still doing crazy stuff. I was still drug dealin'. I was still doing a lot of nonsense, something that didn't really make no sense for me to be doing. So after she told me, I calmed down and just started breaking off from everybody. I was on parole and I got locked up again October 17, 2015 for a violation. Was kicked back out of parole in 2016 on January 15th so that's when I came to St. Leonardo. That's when I told myself enough is enough. I got too much to lose. I got a woman who cares for me. I got a son that needs me, so I can guide him in the right way.

So I just ripped the mask off. I just kicked everybody that didn't mean nothing to me or played a purpose in my life, I just kicked 'em to the curb. Just like coldhearted, I ain't got nothing to do with y'all.

INTERVIEWER: You said the game has changed from before. How's the game changed?

JONATHAN: The game ain't what it used to be. You still got the players, the players are still playing the game, but they going by different rules. They not going by rules that were made in the beginning. What I mean by that is, it's all open doors for everything out there. You see how our fine city is going down in flames? All these kids killing kids, fathers killing kids, mothers killing kids. It's like everything is lost, everybody's lost. I feel like we are in the devil's playground and we're just his puppets right now. The way this city is going hurts me because I used to be a part of the problem and now I'm trying to make steps to help the solution out. Stop all that, stop the violence, cuz there's people that really care about Chicago.

When you get deeper into Chicago where things are really going on and you can see the pain and hurt, the sorriness and the hopelessness of these people out here doing what they're doing, it's like they're lost, they have no guidance. I'm trying to reach out and do what I have to do to help. If I can save one, one can save the next one. I'm tired of seeing people get shot. I'm tired of seeing kids get killed. I'm tired of seeing unnecessary violence. There's no meaning to it.

I'm most proud of making steps to become something I thought I would never be. I thought I would die on the streets. I thought I'd never see the age of eighteen. And I almost lost my life at the age of twenty-six. And now that that happened to me, I don't regret nothing I did in life—nothing—because it helped me become the man I am today. What I learned from these streets I wanna reach out and give the kids. When you go to jail, nobody has your back. Nobody can have you but you or handle you the way you can handle yourself.

INTERVIEWER: From the time you were eleven or so, when you were in gangs and in the streets, you had to be fearless. Now that your life is different and you're trying to help other people, what do you fear now?

JONATHAN: I don't fear nothing. If I gotta die helping somebody out or helping a kid out trying to get 'em off the street, it is what it is. I leave it in God's hands. I don't fear no man, I fear no one. As long as I can help that's all I want. I want to touch the kid. If I can reach and help one kid, that one kid can help the next kid, that kid can help the next one, the next one and the next one. And keep going in that chain reaction so we all can get together as brothers, sisters, fathers, mothers, uncles and all live in peace, not in fear. God's hands. Hopefully, God's got my back.

He did change his life. He accepted Jesus. He was growing into a man of God, and now he is with God. I miss you so much. Rest in peace, my Jonathan.

Sadly, I have lost so many to gun violence that I can't tell all their stories, but I'll never forget my first loss: Johnny Vargas. I met Johnny through a program I worked for in Chicago. This program was required for court-involved, mostly gang-involved, youth to attend as a last option before getting jail time. He and I clicked right away and we became close.

Johnny was funny, warm, and loyal to a fault. Johnny loved the gang lifestyle. His friends would say the same. He was down-to-earth, kindhearted, and caring but also a protector when it came to people he cared about; he was supportive and considerate of others.

One night I had a disturbing dream about Johnny. In the dream he and I were hanging out on a picnic table in the park when two men came up to us and started shooting. Someone grabbed me and ran but left Johnny behind. The whole dream I was trying to find Johnny. Was he dead or alive? Eventually I found him alive. I ran to him and gave him a huge hug, then I woke up. I felt heavy and I knew God was speaking to me, showing me something. I called Johnny and told him about the dream.

"Johnny, God is trying to tell you something," I said. "You're in deep, aren't you?"

"Yeah, very deep," he sighed. "All I can do is try to keep my nephews out. This isn't for everyone . . . and truth is, I don't really want this much anymore."

"Johnny, if you want out, we can do that, but you really need to be safe right now," I said.

Three days later he was shot.

I rushed to the hospital as soon as I heard. He was still fighting for his life. I remembered my dream and thought, he's going to survive. His girlfriend, Jasmine, was at the hospital and told me Johnny had a dream (a couple of days after mine) where he was shot. She said he felt like something was coming and he was being warned.

The doctors came into the waiting room for the family and asked us to leave. I will never get the scream of his mother out of my head when she heard the news. He was gone. I didn't understand. He survived in my dream. That's how it was supposed to end. But it didn't.

Johnny was the first youth I was close to who I lost to gun violence. The only blessing, other than having known Johnny, was the close relationship I developed with his girlfriend afterward. Together we mourn, we remember, we keep living without him.

FIVE THINGS NOT TO SAY

Romans 12:15 says, "Rejoice with those who rejoice; mourn with those who mourn" (NIV). We love to talk about the rejoicing part, but we'd rather leave the mourning to someone else. Though grief is a part of everyday life, walking someone through the grief is not something we're trained for.

How do we help people in grief? How do we help this population of young people who lose friends and gang brothers often? While they often handle their grief through retaliation, how do we help them not become more hardened?

We know that everyone handles grief differently. It's not linear and there's no right or wrong way to feel what you feel. But in trying to help, sometimes our words and actions can actually be quite harmful.

In walking this path often, I have learned (the hard way) not to say the following five things to someone who is grieving:

- **"So, how are you doing?"** I think we pretty much know the answer to that. Instead, say, "I know you're suffering right now." Acknowledge where they are. Acknowledge the pain.

- **"Well, they're in a better place."** How does that truly help the person who is grieving? Instead, say, "I know you must really miss them and you must be hurting."

- **"Please let me know if there is anything I can do for you."** I know this is a statement that has action as its intent, but let's think about this. When I am grieving, I don't even know what I want or what I need. Instead offer concrete things you are going to do, like bring meals, babysit kids, help clean the house, help at the funeral, and so on.

- **"I know how you feel."** You may have had a similar experience, but no two grief experiences are the same. Instead, say, "I can't imagine how you feel right now but I can relate to the pain."

- **"Well, this happens eventually. Death is a part of life."** That's kind of harsh and feels like a brush-off but people say it all the time. Instead, say, "I know this death is so hard to handle. I know you miss them. Tell me something about them."

- **Bonus.** Say nothing at all. Just sit with them in their grief, in the moments. Hold their hand and let them cry.

As ministry workers, we are always in fix-it mode, but when it comes to grief, God does the fixing. The best thing we can do is be present and let people feel what they are feeling. Don't try to fix it, don't use clichés, just be present. Of course, you will be a helping hand, but pay close attention to all that is happening around you: listen, sit in silence holding their hand, pray for them, cry with them, and offer comfort. Be present.

Your presence is most significant when the ceremonies are over and everyone goes back to their everyday life. People are

left trying to figure out life without their loved one while pro-
cessing their grief. These are the most powerful moments to
be present. Two weeks later, you're still bringing a meal. One
month later, you're still visiting. Six months later, you're going
to the grave site with them. Remember, grief is a process and
people go through phases of grieving. Being present through the
phases can bring healing for all involved.

I wish someone would have prepared me for this part of the
ministry . . . and this is my prayer for those who experience this
part of the calling. I'm often asked how I keep going after so
much loss. How was I able to keep going even when I knew I
would be burying more young people? Four things helped me:

God. God kept me. Period. I can't explain his ways or his power
but leaning on him got me through. Psalm 34:18 promises that
the Lord is close to the brokenhearted and saves those who are
crushed in spirit.

Community. The way God kept me the most was through the
community of people who surrounded me and loved me. They
checked on me, brought me food, forced me out of bed into
the shower, went with me to the funerals, were a shoulder to soak
with my tears, became a place to laugh, talk, and wail—my community got me through. My best friends, Tanya, Tiwanda, and
Amanda, were my safe spaces to be totally vulnerable and messy.
They expected nothing from me but gave me all the support I

> WHEN WE ARE GRIEVING, COMMUNITY AND SAFE SPACES ARE ESSENTIAL TO OUR HEALING JOURNEY.

didn't even know I needed. When we are grieving, community and safe spaces are essential to our healing journey.

My young people. Those who suffered the same loss with me gave me strength, and they leaned on me to be their strength. We got through it together, step by step. We were each other's sounding boards. Our bonds were made tighter. Being able to walk *with* them gave me strength and helped me to heal my own pain while helping others heal. We healed together.

Remembering my why. There was a period when I lost three young people within two months. I wanted to give up. The pain and hopelessness were so heavy . . . but when I felt like giving up, I remembered. I remembered God's call on my life. I remembered that I said yes to this ministry and that there were still many youth—who were still alive—who needed me, who I needed. And I also knew that those I lost would be furious with me if I gave up, especially my Jonathan.

The tough part is I know I will bury more young people if I continue in this line of work. I pray against it, but I know it to be true. And I will keep loving these young people until such a time comes. I never want a young person I encounter to die without knowing there is hope . . . and that they were loved—by me, by God.

TWENTY

HOPE IS MY HOMIE

And so, Lord, where do I put my hope?
My only hope is in you.

PSALM 39:7 NLT

Three months after I moved onto Evergreen St., the block in Humboldt Park, one of my youth robbed me.

It was a beautiful Saturday afternoon on the block. One of my youth from G-Phi-G wanted to bless me with dinner and a movie. Before meeting up with him, I drove through the block like I usually do to see who was out and who I could say hello to. I ran into Keeko, who was Luis and Antonio's older brother. He was the only one out on the corner and we chatted for a few. I shared with him that I was headed out to see the new *Avatar*

movie. After chatting for a minute, I headed out to enjoy the rest of my day.

Many hours later, I came home and walked through my front door to a complete wreck of my home. I stood at the door in shock and fear, stuck in place, for what seemed like an eternity. This had never happened to me, and I didn't know what to do. I ran outside and immediately called the police. My landlord, who was with the Chicago PD at the time, showed up with other officers. I was sitting in my car crying, calling my pastor and a few friends to see who could come over to be with me. Several people showed up and offered comfort in a traumatic moment.

I knew who it was: Keeko. He was the only one who knew I would be gone and for a long time (y'all know how long that movie *Avatar* is). He took everything of value to me and more, including my class rings from college and high school. He and his friend even ate some brownies I had just baked that morning. That made me realize they must have been high and probably had the munchies.

The police found no fingerprints and left me with a police report and a messy home to clean up. I was traumatized. My pastor paid for me to stay at a hotel for a couple of nights, which helped a lot, but I knew I had to go back home. Two of my friends came with me when I had to walk through the doors of my robbed home. It didn't feel like home. I felt violated and scared beyond words. My friends helped me clean the house from top to bottom, including washing the sheets the robbers had touched when they flipped the bed. They sat with me for hours until they had to go home. I'll never forget that first night back home alone. I didn't sleep. I was scared, furious, and hurt that Keeko had done that to me after all I had done for him and his family. I couldn't understand how a heart could be so evil with intent to hurt those who are helping you. He will never understand to this day the trauma he left me with. To this very day I still get nervous every time I put the key in the door lock, afraid of what I might see when I open the door.

A week after the robbery, after I wasn't as traumatized, I went to the block and started looking for Keeko. I asked everyone who knew him where he was so I could confront him and maybe get some of my items back. Sounds crazy, I know, but that was who I was. No one had "seen him." No one could point me in his direction. I even went to his gang leader to ask. One of the rules of that gang is you are not supposed to rob your own neighborhood but to protect it. Keeko failed greatly on that one rule, but no action was taken against him and he stayed hidden from me.

Days later, one of the kids came to me as I was sitting on my stoop.

"So, um, Miss Amy," he said with apprehension. "I heard you got robbed. I am so sorry."

"Yeah, it's unfortunate some coward came into my home and stole my stuff," I said. "Really messed me up, man."

"So, um, can I ask you a question?" he asked.

"Always," I said.

"Does this mean you're moving now?" he asked.

"Naw, why would I move?" I replied.

"You sure?" he asked. "What if it happens again?"

"I sure hope it doesn't!" I exclaimed. "But if it does, then I'll handle that too."

"You sure, Miss Amy?" he asked, his body tense.

"Yo, this is my hood too," I said. "I ain't going nowhere."

He exhaled deeply. "That's what's up, Miss Amy. Glad to hear that."

Then we sat and talked for hours.

I went back upstairs to my apartment thinking about our exchange. Why would he ask me if I was moving? Why did he care? It was then I realized what God was doing. These young people, like many youth we deal with, are used to adults coming and going out of their lives. They are not used to mentors, youth leaders, or teachers being around for the long haul. Many young people have had fathers abandon them, friends and family.

Abandonment issues usually happen when "a parent or caregiver does not provide the child with consistent warm or attentive interactions, leaving them feeling chronic stress and fear."[1] This also affects the trust that develops in relationships with adults. So here I was, another adult coming into their lives who they expected to leave. Trust is not given; it is earned . . . and I was here to earn it, no matter what it took. They wanted to know if I was in it for the long haul, if they needed to stop investing in me like I was investing in them.

I'm not saying Keeko robbed me to consciously run me out of town (or did he?), but most of the youth on the block expected me to move afterward. That's what people do when it gets hard—they run. I had something to prove, and this was how I was going to prove it. In my trauma,

> TRUST IS NOT GIVEN; IT IS EARNED . . . AND I WAS HERE TO EARN IT, NO MATTER WHAT IT TOOK.

the youth saw me leaning on the Lord for healing. They saw me leaning on them for community. They saw that hope was their homie.

Soon after, Keeko was arrested for another residential burglary. He admitted to his brother Luis that it was him who robbed me. I have yet to have him talk to me, and he probably never will. But I have forgiven him.

■ ■ ■

It had been years since I had seen Luis and Antonio. I missed having them stop by the house for brownies or running into them on the block. I would occasionally think about them in passing, wondering where they were.

One night I had a dream about both Luis and Antonio. I woke up knowing God wanted me to find them and reach out to them. God has always used my dreams as a way to communicate actions he wants me to take. If God brings someone to mind in a dream or just ordinary life, take the time to reach out to them. It's usually not a coincidence.

I tried to find them on social media. Nothing. I tried to talk to their friends. Nothing. Then, with my heart beating a million miles a minute, I did a search on the Illinois Inmate Search website and found them both. My heart sank, but I was also excited to have found them. I immediately wrote them both a letter, telling them of the dream and my journey to find them. I drove to the post office, kissed the envelopes, and mailed them with hopes they would get the letters quickly. A couple of weeks later, I got a letter from Luis. I was elated! I sat on my porch swing and ripped open the letter.

"I asked God every day to show me a sign that I'm wanted or thought of, so that I can keep pushing and wanting to live another day and feel that I am worthy . . . and then I get mail from you. He really answered my prayers and I'm happy that he is listening to me."

This is how God works and shows off!

■ ■ ■

After being put on his visiting list, I went for my first visit with Luis after many years. I sat anxiously at the little table marked V for visitor, I for inmate, indicating where we should sit. There were several of us waiting for our person to come through the door. Others already had their visitors, many were giggling, kissing, and crying as they greeted their person. I couldn't wait to hug Luis, but would he be okay with that? I didn't care. He was getting a hug!

He walked through the doors, looked around the room, and we connected eye to eye. He checked in and they took him back out of the room. I thought he had been rejected for our visit. I didn't know what was happening. I sat in a quiet panic, and a few minutes later, he walked back through the door. He had to get a complete search (all-clothes-removed inspection) before being able to visit.

As he walked toward me, tears welled up in my eyes. He was now towering over me, muscles and all. He was no longer the youth I met when he was twelve but a young man of twenty-three. We hugged tightly. It'd been a while since he had been hugged and I wanted him to know he was loved through my hug. We sat down. His hands were shaking, and he was sweating on his forehead. His voice was shaky, and he didn't know what to say.

"It's me, Luis," I said as I took his sweaty hand. "It's Amy. You can talk to me, about anything."

"Amy, I'm so sorry for everything," he started as his throat choked up. "You have always been there and I just didn't treat you good. I regret it. I was a kid and, honestly, I wasn't ready to leave the streets. But you were always there. I feel bad but I'm so glad you didn't give up on me."

After that, he calmed down and we had the best four-hour visit talking about everything. We reconnected and our relationship grew. We have since become incredibly close and I no longer consider myself his mentor but his big sister. We are family now.

■ ■ ■

Many youth have come and gone in my life. Some have been heartbreaking losses, while others I can still watch from a distance hoping I made some kind of imprint in their heart even if we don't speak regularly. Many times, when a person moves on from the relationship, we tend to blame ourselves or feel like we have failed them in some way. But I am reminded of the phrase, "Reason, Season, Lifetime." Some people come into your life for a reason, then vanish. Others come for a season, then quietly dip out. And some are there for a lifetime; you can't get rid of them, even if you try. We must have our hearts and hands open to this possibility with every person we come into contact with. My heart breaks that I no longer have Roddy around, but I was only supposed to be there for a season.

This is where trusting God to be God comes in again. I trust I did what God called me to do in that season. I trust God did not abandon Roddy after our relationship ended. I trust God knows what Roddy needs the most and if that doesn't include me, I have to be okay with it. In the end, I want what is best for all my young people, whether that includes me or not.

My pain came as a result of me not trusting God enough with his plan for Roddy, with me taking on the lead role of Roddy's life plan, with me thinking I knew what was best, with me thinking I had failed. When and only when we trust God can we let go and move forward. We pray we made an impact, planted a seed, showed some love and hope . . . and then we let go and move on.

And in some cases, they return, years later, in a dream, at a park, bumping into them at the grocery store, and God says, "This one needs you back during this time." Be open to the ebb and flow of the people in your life, of you in their lives. This is all part of the plan. Trust the plan.

Never never never give up on a person. Never. God never gives up on you.

Too many times I have wanted to, but God reminds me of how he's never given up on me. If you're walking with people in this difficult journey called life, you have to remember the journey's timeline is different for everyone. It's not your timeline. It's a combination of that person's readiness and God's intervention and wisdom.

> NEVER NEVER NEVER GIVE UP ON A PERSON. NEVER. GOD NEVER GIVES UP ON YOU.

A formerly incarcerated youth I'd spent six years mentoring came home from prison. In the last year of his sentence, we'd discussed all his plans to do life differently when he got home. Unfortunately, he decided to do his own thing and go back to the street life . . . and sometimes that happens. Someone can want change with all their heart— and they did change when they were on the inside—but when they get home, they fall back into the old patterns. There is so much anxiety coming home that it's easy to go back to what you know to feel a level of control, comfort, and security. Others are determined to not let that happen to them.

Though it broke my heart, I remained positive. He decided he didn't want me around anymore and cut me off—with no explanation, reason, or conversation. I was devastated and broken. Every two weeks, I would text him to let him know I was thinking about him, praying for him, and that I would never give up on him . . . never one response back.

Finally, after four months of me pursuing him, he texted and said he missed my hugs and wanted to hang out when I got back from out of town. We talked for hours and it was good.

Sometimes young people will cut you off out of shame and embarrassment. Sometimes young people don't know what it means for someone to stay consistent, even after they try to hurt you and ditch you. Sometimes young people think if they hurt you, it's an excuse for you to give up on them permanently.

Yes, most people don't understand the love of God—I'm still learning. But that's why we can't give up . . . because he never does. Pursue them with the love that God has pursued you with. It can make all the difference.

Of all the people I have loved, walked life with, served, and ministered to, my favorite story is still that of my baby brother. After such a traumatic childhood, years in out of the gang and prison and a lifestyle of addiction, my brother finally hit rock bottom and decided this wasn't the life he was meant to live. He wanted a better, healthy life. He reconnected with the love of his life, Amanda, left Los Angeles, and they started a new life together. They married in 2016 and have a beautiful daughter, Samantha Amber, my bestie niece. He now owns his own business and is living a full, happy life. I know few people who can survive what he has and create a healthy life. I am beyond proud. This is what happens when you *see* people, labor in prayer, and don't give up on them.

And so, Lord, where do I put my hope?
My only hope is in you. (Psalm 39:7 NLT)

Hope is the answer. And our hope is in the Lord.

But how can we give an answer to someone who needs hope if they don't see hope in our lives? It begins with God but shines through you. The Lord is the object of our hope. He is our anchor in a restless sea. Our hope is found in the God who sees us, knows us, loves us, and has a plan for us. If you don't serve a God who holds you in the palm of his hands, a God who tenderly cares for you as a child, a God who is involved in every aspect of your life, a God who whispers in those dark times, "I am here with you," a God who finds you in darkness, grabs your hand, and brings you to the light, hope is difficult to come by. But you can know this God for yourself. Don't go another day without hope. And with that hope, you can be a light in someone's darkness.

In this journey of seeing others, we are blessed to see ourselves as well. We have the unique opportunity to embrace how God sees us and in turn see others. With this new lens, we gain compassion for those others ignore. And compassion causes us to act, changing the world and touching lives God deeply cares for and loves. I pray this journey has expanded your worldview, softened your heart, and made your heart burst alive as you see others through the eyes of God.

ACKNOWLEDGMENTS

When I count my blessings, I count you twice.

I truly want to thank those I love for believing in me, but it starts (and ends) with him. God, there are no words to humbly express my gratefulness. You have proven your love and faithfulness to me time and time again. May the words on these pages make you a proud Daddy.

I am no one without my family.

Daddy, I still can't believe you're not here, and you won't be reading my book. When I wanted to give up, I heard you saying, like you always did, "Get back to writing." I finished this for and because of you. My heart is forever broken without you here. I miss you so deeply, Daddy. Until we meet again, forever a Daddy's girl.

Mom, you always believed I would do big things. Thank you for being the strongest woman I know. I am who I am because of your strength, guidance, and love. I love you beyond words.

To my baby brother, Khalil, this is for you too. Hope I made you proud of me, like I am of you. There are no words in the dictionary that can explain how much I love you. You already know, more! Never that.

To my beautiful niece Samantha, Auntie Amy loves you more than I ever thought I could love anyone. You give me life and a love that fills my whole heart. I love watching life through your eyes. You are my world, Pookie Pookie. I'm always here for you! Besties for life!

To my niece Amber, you aren't here to see this, but I know you're with me. You were the first example of God's unconditional love when I needed to know what that looked like. You are still that light to me. RIP my baby girl.

To my nephew Quran, I miss and love you . . . more than you know.

Willow, I've known you for as long as I can remember, and I thank God you've always been in my life. I adore and love you deeply. Family forever, got it?

Joseph, I am so thankful for you. You make my mom so happy . . . and I love you for that.

To my three best friends who have helped me navigate this life—and this book! Tiwanda, Tanya, and Amanda, I never wanted a sister, but God gave me three. Never knew I needed ones like you three.

Tiwanda, thirty-one years together. You were the best bestest sista friend I ever had. Life looks so different without you here. I know you're with me, but I miss you beyond words. I'll see you again, sis . . . you better be at the Gate waiting with a hug.

Tanya, you are my bestie soul mate sista friend beyond eternity . . . and further than that. Thank you for being my biggest cheerleader. You are wonderfully one of a kind! My love for you is forever . . . and longer than that!

Thank you, Tanya and Tiwanda, for never giving up on me. Y'all kept me a Christian!

Amanda, I never could have prayed for a better sister-in-love, wife for my brother, and momma to my niece. You really are the best. Always (whatever that means).

I am so thankful for the InterVarsity Press team. IVP, you were such an amazing team to work with. Thank you for making me feel like a rock star with a purpose! Al Hsu, you held my hand through this journey (and before). You challenged me and I learned and grew and became a better author. Thank you for believing in this project. Nilwona Nowlin, you've been a good friend for many years, and I thank you for everything you did to launch this project. To the Voices team, Leroy and Donna Barber, y'all are just amazing (besides that Dallas/Eagle thing, #NE-Patriots4Life).

To my special cheerleaders who believed in me all the way from the very beginning, when it was just a dream, to the written product: Dan Short, Theresa Morales Soloma, Colleen Smith, Tania Nuñez, Kathy Khang, Irene Cho, Anne Dean, Pastah Jonathan Brooks, Margot Lamar Starbuck, Don Kauffman, Jazmine Torres, and everyone who prayed for me!

I want to share my deep appreciation for those I consider to be my mentors: Pastor Phil Jackson, Carol Sato, Scott Larson, and several others who impacted my life and ministry. "You cannot teach a man anything. You can only help him to find it within himself," (Galileo Galilei). Thank you for helping me discover who God created me to be, for telling me the truth and teaching me so much!

And just because I love and appreciate you so much for so many reasons: St. Anthony Lloyd, Ivette Vazquez-Melendez, Aida Rosario, Jose Velez, my godson Isaiah Lyons, Tehron Cates, Megan McDermott Fountain, Kenny Lee, my three favorite cousins—Danielle, Roy, and Darius. Big love to Lisette, Mikey G., and Fer Fer.

Special shout-out and a lot of love to some of my IYC (and former IYC) youth: Coley Cole, Govanni, Hernan, San Diego,

Rivera, Mello, Cortez, Rush, Durr, Contreras, Cristian . . . and also Andrew, Angel, Sergio . . . and many more not mentioned here. To all my Beach and Spaulding youth (too many to name), I simply adore you! You changed my life. I'm profoundly humbled.

And to the many youth I have lost to gun violence. You didn't deserve it and this world isn't the same without you. It's a loss, not only to me and your families but to our community, to this world.

I am so thankful to be associated with the DVULI family, the UYWI family, the CCDA family, the New Life Centers and IDJJ family, the HOPE Squad team, Christ CREW, the ECC family, the North Park University family, the UNC-Chapel Hill family (GDTBAT), and the Ben L. Smith High School family (Eagle Pride!). What an impact you've had on my life!

To many others (especially my FB fam—you know who you are), I am thankful for but can't name you all! I have not forgotten your love and support.

And to my favorite oversized black hoodie that gave me comfort, warmth, and a homelike feeling when writing with *Martin* episodes playing in the background.

Mostly to all the young people I have been blessed to love and walk life with—I can't name you all. You have changed my life forever and I am thankful for that. Praying that in some way you saw God's love and experienced his hope. Never lose hope. Never give up. And always know you are valued and loved.

Thank you again, my beautiful Lord and Savior.

NOTES

PREFACE

[1] James Forman Jr., "Justice Springs Eternal," *New York Times*, March 25, 2017, https://www.nytimes.com/2017/03/25/opinion/sunday/justice-springs -eternal.html.

1. THE GOD WHO SEES

[1] Miguel De La Torre, *Doing Christian Ethics from the Margins* (Maryknoll, NY: Orbis, 2014), 33.

[2] Jae M. Sevelius et al., "Research with Marginalized Communities: Challenges to Continuity During the COVID-19 Pandemic," *AIDS and Behavior* 24, no. 7 (May 2020): 2009-12.

[3] *The Longman Dictionary of Contemporary English*, s.v. "on the margin," accessed December 5, 2023, www.ldoceonline.com/dictionary/on-the-margin-s.

[4] De La Torre, *Doing Christian Ethics*, 31.

[5] "Sawubona!" Loom International, accessed October 19, 2023, www.loominter national.org/sawubona.

[6] "Sawubona!" Loom International.

[7] Kasey Van Norman, *Hagar Bible Study Guide: In the Face of Rejection, God Says I'm Significant* (Grand Rapids, MI: Zondervan, 2019), 13.

[8] Jim Melanson, *Hagar of Egypt: A Perspective on Strength, Courage & Faith* (self-pub., 2017), 61.

[9] Melanson, *Hagar of Egypt*, 62.

2. BEST OF BOTH WORLDS

[1] Christian Milneil, "Maine's Slow Gains in Racial Diversity," *Portland Press Herald*, https://www.pressherald.com/interactive/interactive-map-maines -slow-gains-racial-diversity, accessed October 21, 2023.

4. TO BE SEEN OR NOT TO BE SEEN

[1] Matthew Brown, "Father's Faith: Perceptions of God May Stem from Dad-Child Relationship," *Washington Times*, June 15, 2013, https://www.washington times.com/news/2013/jun/15/fathers-faith-perceptions-god-may-stem-dad -child-r.

5. A DIFFERENT KINDA CHRISTIAN

[1]Lecrae, "I'm Turnt," *Church Clothes Vol. 2*, Reach Records, 2013.
[2]Lecrae, "I'm Turnt."

6. LETHAL ABSENCE OF HOPE

[1]Gregory Boyle, on *Dr. Phil*, "Father Greg Boyle of Homeboy Industries Gives Hope to Troubled Kids," hosted by Phil McGraw, aired December 14, 2010.
[2]Boyle, *Dr. Phil*, "Father Greg Boyle."
[3]Boyle, *Dr. Phil*, "Father Greg Boyle."

7. THE BUSINESS OF SEEING OTHERS

[1]Gregory Boyle, on *Dr. Phil*, "Father Greg Boyle of Homeboy Industries Gives Hope to Troubled Kids," hosted by Phil McGraw, aired December 14, 2010.
[2]Wes Angelozzi (@wes_angelozzi), Instagram post, October 3, 2015, www.instagram.com/p/8YtNArNIrS/.
[3]Max Lucado, *Just Like Jesus* (book promotional page), copyright 2023, https://maxlucado.com/products/just-like-jesus.
[4]Gregory Boyle, *Tattoos on the Heart: The Power of Boundless Compassion* (New York: Free Press, 2010), 67.

8. THE PRIVILEGE OF PRESENCE

[1]Stacy Weiner, "Bryan Stevenson: It's Time to Change the Narrative Around Race and Poverty," AAMC, November 8, 2019, www.aamc.org/news/Bryan-stevenson-it-s-time-change-narrative-around-race-and-poverty.

10. IT'S NOT ABOUT FIXING PEOPLE

[1]Robert D. Lupton, *Theirs Is the Kingdom: Celebrating the Gospel in Urban America*, ed. Barbara R. Thompson (New York: Harper Collins, 1989), 6.
[2]Gregory Boyle, *Tattoos on the Heart: The Power of Boundless Compassion* (New York: Free Press, 2010), 188.
[3]Lupton, *Theirs Is the Kingdom*, 6.
[4]Heather Gingrich, *Restoring the Shattered Self: A Christian Counselor's Guide to Complex Trauma* (Downers Grove, IL: InterVarsity Press, 2013), 17.
[5]Martin Taylor, "What Does Fight, Flight, Freeze, Fawn Mean?" WebMD, April 28, 2022, https://www.webmd.com/mental-health/what-does-fight-flight-freeze-fawn-mean.
[6]Gingrich, *Restoring the Shattered Self*, 20.
[7]R. Dandridge Collins, *The Trauma Zone: Trusting God for Emotional Healing* (Chicago: Lift Every Voice, 2007), 14.

[8]The National Child Traumatic Stress Network, "Trauma in the Lives of Gang Involved Youth: Tips for Volunteers and Community Organizations," www .nctsn.org/sites/default/files/resources/tip-sheet/trauma_in_the_lives_of _gang_involved_youth_volunteers_community_organizations.pdf, accessed October 28, 2023.

12. MENTORING THAT MATTERS

[1]Mentoring Partnership of Southwestern PA, "Mentor Guidelines and Code of Conduct," accessed October 29, 2023, www.mentoringpittsburgh.org/rails /active_storage/blobs/eyJfcmFpbHMiOnsibWVzc2FnZSI6IkJBaHBBBZ2NCI iwiZXhwIjpudWxsLCJwdXIiOiJibG9iX2lkIn19--ad4882277511066cd52e9b5 5971c8a2253c68962/TMP_Mentor_Code_of_Conduct.doc.

[2]Jennifer Herrity, "Qualities of a Good Listener and How To Be One in 6 Steps," Indeed, February 3, 2023, https://www.indeed.com/career-advice/career -development/good-listening.

13. WHAT I'VE LEARNED ABOUT GANG MEMBERS AND GANG CULTURE

[1]"Video: Why Youth Join Gangs," National Gang Center, U.S. Department of Justice, https://nationalgangcenter.ojp.gov/video, accessed November 5, 2023.

[2]Mike Ramey, workshop handout (NGCRC 26th International Gang Specialist Training, National Gang Crime Research Center, Chicago, July 31 to August 2, 2023).

14. LAND OF THE FREE? INCARCERATION NATION

[1]Wendy Sawyer and Peter Wagner, "Mass Incarceration: The Whole Pie 2023," Prison Policy Initiative, March 14, 2023, www.prisonpolicy.org/reports /pie2023.html.

[2]Sawyer and Wagner, "Mass Incarceration."

[3]Quoted in Amy Williams, "The Visits," *I Am a Hope Dealer* blog, January 22, 2012, https://thehopedealer.wordpress.com/2012/01/22/the-visits/.

[4]Quoted in Williams, "The Visits."

[5]Quoted in Williams, "The Visits."

[6]Craig Haney, "From Prison to Home: The Effect of Incarceration and Reentry on Children, Families, and Communities," Assistant Secretary for Planning and Evaluation, Department of Health and Human Services, November 30, 2001, https://aspe.hhs.gov/reports/psychological-impact-incarceration -implications-post-prison-adjustment-0.

[7] Haney, "From Prison to Home."

[8] Haney, "From Prison to Home."

[9] Haney, "From Prison to Home."

15. THE GREAT I AM . . . *NOT*

[1] Michael LeFebvre, "'I Am Who I Am'? The Real Meaning of God's Name in Exodus," Center for Hebraic Thought, February 15, 2022, https://hebraic thought.org/meaning-of-gods-name-i-am-exodus.

16. EMBRACING YOUR CALLING

[1] Frederick Buechner, *Wishful Thinking: A Seeker's ABC* (New York: Harper & Row, 1973), 95.

[2] Quoted in Brittini L. Palmer, "The Key to Howard Thurman's Spirituality Is 'What Makes You Come Alive,'" *Sojourners*, March 14, 2023, https://sojo.net /articles/key-howard-thurman-s-spirituality-what-makes-you-come-alive.

17. THE GIFT OF BROKENNESS

[1] Bryan Stevenson, *Just Mercy: A Story of Justice and Redemption* (New York: Spiegel & Grau, 2014), 17.

[2] Henri J. M. Nouwen, *The Wounded Healer: Ministry in Contemporary Society* (Garden City, NY: Doubleday & Co., 1972), 93.

18. BUILDING TOGETHER THROUGH TEACHABLE MOMENTS

[1] Maya Angelou, *Oh Pray My Wings Are Gonna Fit Me Well* (New York: Bantam Books 1975), 18.

19. DEATH ALMOST KILLED ME

[1] Adapted from a video-recorded interview and edited for space.

20. HOPE IS MY HOMIE

[1] Smitha Bhandari, "Abandonment Issues: Symptoms and Signs," WebMD, December 12, 2022, www.webmd.com/mental-health/abandonment-issues -symptoms-signs.

ABOUT THE AUTHOR

 **Amy L. Williams** ministers to teens involved in gangs and those lost in the criminal justice system using a key strategy of life-on-life mentoring. As a certified gang intervention specialist, she heard God's call to move into a Latino gang neighborhood in Chicago's Humboldt Park community to be a "hope dealer" doing street outreach and walking life with young people on her block. Amy is project coordinator at New Life Centers, bringing restorative justice programming to youth at juvenile prisons. Amy has been a youth pastor, a reentry coordinator, and a youth mentor and advocate. She is a graduate of both the University of North Carolina at Chapel Hill and National Louis University. She resides in Chicago, loves salsa dancing, and is a true beach baby.
www.ahopedealer.org

ABOUT THE CCDA

IVP is pleased to partner with the Christian Community Development Association (CCDA) to publish a line of co-branded books that align with both organizations' shared values of justice and community development. Founded under the leadership of Dr. John Perkins more than thirty years ago, CCDA aims to inspire, train, and connect Christians who seek to bear witness to the Kingdom of God by reclaiming and restoring under-resourced communities. All the authors of books in this collection are CCDA members and practitioners, and most have held leadership positions within the organization and are nationally recognized experts in the work of Christian community development.
www.ccda.org/ivp

THE VOICES PROJECT

The Voices Project gathers leaders of color who influence culture (the church, education, art, entertainment, politics, and business) for important conversations about the current challenges and triumphs within communities of color and our role as cultural influencers. We train and promote leaders of color to offer voice to culture and society.

TRAINING AND PROMOTING

We provide insight on how to be effective in leadership within one's respective area of cultural influence in a way that is rooted in history and experience of people of color. Additionally we connect leaders of color to leadership opportunities that are based in their areas of expertise within a domain of cultural influence.

INITIATIVES

- Mentorship or small group training with Voices staff (ongoing)
- Publishing company (ongoing)
- Bi-annual leadership gathering (January and August)
- Voices Conference (May)
- Northwestern college tour (October)
- Monthly newsletter (ongoing)

THE VOICES PROJECT
255 SW Bluff Dr
Bend, OR 97702
http://www.voices-project.org/

 https://twitter.com/jointhevoices

 https://www.facebook.com/JoinTheVoices/

 https://www.instagram.com/jointhevoices/